4-
X LIB

WITHDRAWN

D1601238

The
First Air Race

OWEN S. LIEBERG

The
First Air Race

*The International Competition
at Reims, 1909*

Doubleday & Company, Inc.
Garden City, New York   1974

JEFFERSON MADISON REGIONAL
LIBRARY CHARLOTTESVILLE VA

TL
721.6
G7
L5
1974

NATURAL HISTORY MUSEUM
OF library
LOS ANGELES COUNTY

797.5
Lieberg

Library of Congress Cataloging in Publication Data

Lieberg, Owen S
    The first air race; the international competition at Reims, 1909.

    Bibliography
    1. Grande semaine d'aviation de Champagne, Reims, 1909.
2. Gordon Bennett aviation cup. I. Title.
TL721.6.G7L5   797.5′2′094432
ISBN 0-385-07230-9
Library of Congress Catalog Card Number 73–83649

Copyright © 1974 by Doubleday & Company, Inc.
All Rights Reserved
Printed in the United States of America
First Edition

Acknowledgments

I am very grateful for the interest and help given me by so many friends in the journalistic and aeronautical worlds without whose generous assistance I would have found it difficult, if not impossible, to write this narrative of the Reims Flying Week.

In particular, I am indebted to A. W. L. Naylor, librarian of the Royal Aeronautical Society; E. Strachan, wing commander, and John Blake, of the United Service and Royal Aero Club, London, England; Sally Hart and Eva Cress, for secretarial help; Gladys and Elan Lieberg, for introductions and personal co-operation; Louis S. Casey, National Air and Space Division, Smithsonian Institution, for advice; Christine Jones, for her work in translating data and relevant information from the original "Reims Program"; and Miss Tilbury, of *Flight International*, for her co-operation in my research of early records. I also thank Colonel Rougevin-Baville, *conservateur* of the Musée de l'Air, for his help in selecting original photographs of the Reims meeting.

I appreciate the help given by the following institutions: San Diego Aerospace Museum, San Diego, California; National Air and Space Museum, Smithsonian Institution, Washington, D.C.; Science Museum, Aeronautics Division, London, England; Library of Congress, Washington, D.C.; British Museum, London, England; and Brown Brothers Ltd., London, England (for photographs).

I am indebted to the following publishers for permission to refer to several of their publications used in my research on early flying: Putnam and Company Ltd., London, England; and the Blandford Press Ltd., London, England, and Kenneth Munson, *Pioneer Aircraft,* with particular reference to the illustrations by John Wood.

Contents

Contents

The
First Air Race

A Rainy Morning

"Is that *The Golden Flyer?*" asked James Gordon Bennett. "Those few packages?"

The enterprising publisher of the New York *Herald* looked incredulously at the small assembly of crates and boxes which Glenn Curtiss and his mechanics had just unloaded from the S.S. *Savoie*. The whole lot could be packed into the open motorcar which stood nearby at dockside. The largest package was that of the two wooden propellers; even the engine was contained in one small crate.

"I don't give much for America's chances in the speed trophy race," Gordon Bennett continued, referring to the race which he would be sponsoring and to the magnificent solid silver trophy which he had donated together with a prize of $5,000 for the pilot of the fastest airplane in the world. The race was two weeks away.

Flying, then in its infancy in 1909, was drawing the finest pilots to France to compete in a week of flying, inaugurated by the city of Reims and made possible by the generous offer of money prizes given by the great champagne growers of France, Moët and Chandon, Heidsieck, Veuve Clicquot, G. H. Mumm, Pommery, and all the others. Never before had there been such a competition. Never before had there been so much international prestige at stake.

Cortlandt Field Bishop, president of the Aero Club of America, shook his head gravely. He, too, had expected more than this, at least a complete airplane lashed to the deck of the *Savoie,* as deck cargo, but these few packages? It was more than he could understand. He had tried to get the Wright brothers to compete at Reims, but they had refused for various reasons and left Cortlandt Bishop no choice but to ask Curtiss to come over and compete. Curtiss had built the plane secretly at his factory in Hammondsport, New York, but having no time to test it and prove its airworthiness, had dismantled it, and here it was in France, in several small but compact packages ready to be taken to the racetrack outside Reims, near the small village of Bétheny.

"So this is the Glenn Curtiss whom you were so keen to bring over," observed Gordon Bennett as he watched the gaunt figure of the younger man, checking the crates a dozen yards away. "He is not very impressive in appearance, not like Blériot or Farman. Let's hope he can fly. He's up against the best French fliers, the finest in the world, and he's only got a few days in which to get to Reims, unpack and assemble, test and fly his airplane, and be ready for the first day. I can't see him making it. . . . Has he only the one airplane?"

Gordon Bennett gave another glance at the uneffusive-looking American who looked more like a mechanic than an aircraft designer and a director of the Herring-Curtiss Company. "If only he looked the part. . . ."

"Forget his looks," replied Cortlandt Bishop. "He'll surprise them all when he gets into the air. This Glenn Curtiss has a good record. He has already won several races, and I rate him as good as any who will be at Reims."

"Everything's against him," replied Gordon Bennett. "He's only got a few days in which to assemble his airplane and get it into the air before the meeting starts. I'll be surprised if he makes it." Bennett shrugged his shoulders as he spoke and turned away, disappointed with what he had seen. With obvious dismay the two men got into their automobile and were soon heading south toward Paris and the medieval city of Reims.

There were to be eleven contestants for the Gordon Bennett International Aviation Trophy, but only two of these would give it an international interest. G. B. Cockburn, from England, and Curtiss, from the United States. The Italian Lieutenant Mario Calderara had found it impossible to attend—leaving France to provide by far the greatest number of pilots.

Apart from the Gordon Bennett Cup, the long-distance and endurance Grand Prix would be the most attractive event of the meet. For this contest, which would be flown daily until the final day's reckoning, the prize money was $20,000. With increasing excitement it was hoped that one day's record would be beaten the next. Endurance was something that the pilots of 1909 were lacking. Never before had anyone been able to stay in the air for more than three hours, and indeed few had stayed aloft for over one hour. Even Louis Blériot, with his cross-Channel flight behind him, had never flown for more than thirty-five minutes.

The pilots at Bétheny were hoping for good weather to break the long-distance record which Roger Sommer held. He had flown for 2 hours 27 minutes 15 seconds in a Farman biplane, and this was the world record. Louis Paulhan in his Voisin-built biplane had managed to stay aloft for

only 1 hour 32 minutes, and of all the others only Paul
Tissandier in a Wright, Henri Farman in his own biplane,
and Hubert Latham in an Antoinette monoplane had ever
exceeded one hour in the air in continuous flying. Physical
fitness and determination played a great part in those early
endurance flights. The pilot sat in the open without protection, facing a wind relative to his speed of 50 to 60 miles
an hour, with rain or hail to add to the numbing effects on
a man's body. These could be hardships not easily overcome.

Flying machines could not stay in the air in strong winds,
and the buffeting that any light craft could stand was
limited. Yet strangely enough it was not the airplane that
failed but the engine that most often brought the pilot to
the ground against his will. Motors in those days were not
always reliable, and mechanical failures were more likely
than problems with the structural members. Everyone expected Sommer to take the honors in this race at the ex-
pense of Paulhan, the major challenger, but prophecies
have a habit of failing and Reims would be no exception.

Saturday, August 21, 1909, was a day of despair for the
hopes of everyone. It had rained heavily all the previous
day, and the racecourse at Bétheny was still flooded in parts,
particularly near the grandstands and the area reserved for
motorcars and standing spectators. The new roads were in
a shocking state, with pools of water everywhere by night-
fall, and the road leading to the grandstands and airplane
hangars was almost impassable by that Friday evening.
Motorcars delivering stores and airplane parts had sunk to
their axles in the mud. Many feared that if conditions did
not improve, the meeting might have to be abandoned. As
it was getting dark, truckloads of ashes and stones were
hurriedly brought to the racecourse to prevent a quagmire.

The prologue for Reims was not a happy one; in a few

hours flying was due to start. Last-minute problems had
been expected, but to be faced with such bad weather and
the possibility of a canceled meeting was too much for the
organizers. It was an astonishing sight, therefore, that
greeted the officials on Sunday, August 22. In spite of the
rain, hundreds of spectators trudged hopefully along the
roads toward the line of grandstands that could be seen beyond the trees. They came from all directions—an unusual
sight for a Sunday, a day of rest or church services and
then relaxation. Men and women were streaming toward
the racetrack on the plains of Bétheny to see these new flying machines at the first aviation meeting ever to be held in
Europe, "La Grande Semaine d'Aviation de la Champagne."

The flimsy machines of wood and canvas had been arriving at the racecourse during the past week, brought by their
makers and accompanied by pilots whose names were already making household news. The newspapers had reported the arrival of international figures, politicians, and
statesmen. They had been describing the lives of the pilots
and the builders of these new heavier-than-air contraptions,
these "flying machines." They had been relating stories of
man's persistent struggle to overcome the elements and defeat the forces that kept them on the ground. Headlines
told how man could emulate the birds and fly. For days,
the main topic in cafés and homes, in the street and in the
factories, had been flying and the forthcoming meeting.

The distant towers of Reims Cathedral were obscured by
low cloud. The roads leading to the racecourse were being
churned into mud. The chalky mess, after days of rain, was
still ankle deep in many places. Near the grandstands
wooden planks had been placed, and walking was a little
easier, although still precarious. Many of the enthusiasts
had been walking since daybreak and even before, while

some came in horse-drawn vehicles of every type. There
was a surprising number of the more affluent, who were arriving in cars that were as uncertain as the flying machines
their occupants hoped to see. All were making their way
slowly toward Bétheny. Some of the cars became stuck in
the mud and had to be pulled out by horses, a somewhat
bizarre spectacle in a world now entering this new era of
mechanical flight.

At the door of one of the hangars a man still in his twen-
ties stood gazing across the wet, soggy field at the scene before him. Gabriel Voisin watched the rain falling and the
distant trees swaying in the wind. Here and there were a
few forlorn figures, wet but still optimistic enough to seek
shelter wherever they could. He watched them without interest, depressed and worried. They were just part of a dull,
gloomy landscape. A week before his hopes could not have
been higher—but now, with the howling wind and driving
rain, his spirits were at their lowest ebb. Doubts pervaded
him. At that moment, on that early August morning, it
seemed as though the flying would have to be abandoned.

Nagging thoughts assailed him. What if this wind and
rain continued for the entire week? It could be the end of
all their hopes. For months he had been waiting for this
day, when his and other men's planes would be soaring
over the Bétheny fields to show a doubting world the progress which aviation had made. For weeks the newspapers
had been filling their columns with the prowess of the few
brave men who took up frail assemblies of wood and canvas, held together with wooden struts and bracing wires.
Now it seemed the wind would keep them grounded, and
frustrated men would have to watch in despair while a disappointed public coming in the thousands would gradually
lose interest. The excited and keen enthusiasts could become bitter and resentful. In one day, if there was no flying,

all their hopes could be dashed in defeat; there was no telling what could follow.

Someone came from behind him and was speaking. "Is the rain going to stop, Monsieur Voisin? Will there be any flying this morning?"

Voisin turned to the speaker who had joined him at the hangar entrance. It was his chief mechanic in oil-stained overalls, his dirty hands holding a ball of rags with which he was attempting to wipe off the grease, but without much success.

"Flying? No hope of that yet. This rain"—he paused—"could keep up all day—and the wind, too. We can't fly in this wind, and if we don't, these people"—he waved his hands widely—"aren't going to be pleased."

"It is not raining as much as it was earlier," the mechanic observed as he stepped outside the hangar and held out one hand hopefully.

"I don't mean the rain; it is the wind, this gale, that worries me. We can fly in the rain but not in this wind." Voisin half turned toward the other. "It will only take one bad crash and someone like Blériot or Farman to get hurt"—he shrugged his shoulders in despair—"or killed, and the meeting will be finished." He gave a final look at the forlorn scene and as he turned his back on it, reiterated, "Finished. C'est fini."

The mechanic, still wiping his hands, followed him, shaking his head sadly. It was true, he realized: The success of Reims depended on one thing, the weather. If the wind increased, if an impatient flier, risking the treacherous gusts, took off too soon and crashed, there could be trouble. The French crowds of those early years of the twentieth century had unpredictable moods when frustrated or disappointed. They had paid good francs to see flying machines, and they would want to see them flying.

An hour passed, the rain was a mere drizzle now, and men were venturing beyond the protection of the covered stands. A small group, obviously officials, moved quickly from one shed to another.

The enthusiasm of the crowd was not dampened, even if their clothes were ruined by the torrential downpour. At that moment in the early morning they were still optimistic. The setting was unusual. The eager feeling of those in the covered stands was infectious. They had come a long way; they had been promised a week of flying, something nobody had ever seen before. They were going to enjoy themselves even if the wind was howling about their ears and the rain was still pouring down. They were not concerned with the dangers such weather could do to the frail craft now in the protection of the hangars. Those in the grandstands could not care less; these lucky ones were comfortable in their seats, and nothing else mattered. Occasionally the roar of an engine inside one of the sheds vied with the gale outside.

As the day grew lighter and the grandstands gradually filled, not only did the rain stop but the wind lessened, and at last there was hope for better conditions. A black flag still flew at the top of the pylon across the field—not far from the judges' box—to signify "no flying." A few gendarmes strolled unconcernedly in front of the stands ignoring the few spectators who had wandered onto the field.

Two men, walking briskly, crossed the track and entered the shed where Voisin had been standing not long before. They passed inside but reappeared almost immediately, accompanied by the young veteran flier. They walked onto the racecourse, clutching their programs and other papers in one hand and holding on to their hats with the other. One was dressed in pilot's overalls, the other in the dark jacket and striped trousers of an official. He was speaking to Voisin.

"We think flying could start, Monsieur Voisin."

"There is still a risk in this wind, Monsieur Archdeacon. If Blériot wants to risk his life, that's his business. He is a good pilot, but he takes risks. There are others who are not so experienced. If anyone is killed, flying will have to stop, and we have many who have not had Blériot's good luck." He turned to the other man in the clean overalls of a well-dressed pilot. "Don't you agree, Captain Ferber?"

Ferdinand Ferber shook his head. "I don't think the wind is too bad. Esnault-Pelterie does not think so either."

Voisin thought for a while, then nodded slowly as he gave grudging assent. That done, he turned on his heel and without another word walked back into the hangar. Captain Ferber watched him with a grim smile. "What are we waiting for?" he commented. "Let us start flying."

Within a few minutes the quiet atmosphere around the judges' box changed. Men hurried toward the pylon which also served as a flagstaff. The little group of men were gesticulating to each other wildly as one of them took hold of the signal ropes. Down came the black flag, and for a moment there was silence everywhere. Then three other signal flags took its place and fluttered slowly to the top. A cheer went up across the ground as an excited crowd watched a white disk, a red pointed pennant and a white rectangle give the official declaration.

"Attention! Flights are about to commence."

Cheering broke out as a slow-moving procession emerged from the dark, cavernous interior of one of the sheds that bordered the field. Drawn by a solitary horse, escorted by two of the gendarmes and a small group of men, mechanics and helpers, the first of the flying machines appeared. It was a monoplane, known as R.E.P., designed and built by

Robert Esnault-Pelterie. It was a curious-looking machine with two bicycle wheels under the tail plane at the rear. It was painted a bright red. To prevent damage to the wing, each tip was fitted with a smaller bicycle wheel so placed that should either wing dip, the wheel would take the main shock. The 35-horsepower 7-cylinder air-cooled R.E.P. engine drove a four-bladed propeller. Its external bracing wires were common to all monoplanes of this period. A wooden skid or runner was used to keep the plane from tipping forward and the propeller from hitting the ground on landing.

The R.E.P. was wheeled slowly across the field as a feeling of excitement rippled through the crowded grandstands. After hours of waiting, at times in lethargic despair, the sight of the red monoplane stirred the crowds with hopeful anticipation.

It reached the starting point and was moved into position to take off down the field in front of the grandstands. Since Esnault-Pelterie was suffering from an injured hand, one of his crew was to substitute as pilot. He climbed into the wooden seat as the remaining mechanics took up their positions around the monoplane. One stood at each wing tip, two were holding down the tail, while Esnault-Pelterie stood behind the chief mechanic who had taken hold of the propeller. As Esnault-Pelterie gripped his chief mechanic by the shoulders, the latter slowly and nonchalantly swung the propeller for a few turns. The crowds were stilled, waiting expectantly; even the wind dropped and added to the strange peace that seemed to pervade the entire racetrack.

In those early years swinging a propeller to start the engine was a dangerous procedure. When possible, two and sometimes three mechanics would be needed. There would be one to swing and the other (or others) to pull the front man away from the spinning propeller and out of danger once the engine had started.

As the crowd waited, they heard the pilot shout and saw the mechanic give the propeller a quick, vicious swing, this time with a determined grunt, before jumping to one side. A short spluttering sound followed as the engine roared into speed. The pilot "revved up" the engine, and soon the propeller was spinning at top speed. At the rear of the monoplane, hats were flying in the man-made gale and men were shouting as the tail tried to rise. Then, as Esnault-Pelterie and his chief mechanic leaped aside, the pilot raised a gloved hand and the men released their hold on the quivering plane. It slowly edged forward, bumping its way over the field and gathering speed as it traveled down the course, but it refused to fly. The cheers that greeted its first movement died down until there was a strange silence. The crowd watched the monoplane rock its way across the ground, its throttle wide open, followed by Esnault-Pelterie and two of his crew, waiting hopefully for it to leave the ground.

Esnault-Pelterie's monoplane looked like a huge bird with its wings outstretched, fluttering along the field, tilting first one way and then the other. Two more attempts to rise into the air followed without success. Groans could be heard across the field and jeering shouts came from the crowded stands. Was this what they had come all the way to see? If this was all the organizers could do, why all the big prizes? Their annoyed feelings spread quickly, and this was turning to intense bitterness. Suddenly, groans stopped as quickly as they had begun; another machine was being pulled out of another hangar toward the starting line. The attitude of the crowd softened; there was a feeling of relief. Maybe this one would do better.

The second plane, unlike the first, was a biplane. It had

no wheels but was carried on a trolley. The crowd watched with keen interest as the Wright biplane was lifted onto the specially built steel track. It was almost eleven o'clock as Paul Tissandier climbed into the pilot's seat and took hold of the controls. A few adjustments, a wave of the hand, and the machine was sliding along the track before rising swiftly into the air. The crowd was happy—the flying machine was actually flying. At last they were seeing the first of the airplanes which the newspapers had been describing for so long. No wonder they were excited, no wonder they cheered.

But their excitement was short-lived. The shouting stopped and gave way to despair again when the engine began to stutter into a series of tired coughs. The misfiring continued for a few seconds until even that stopped and the crowds watched in silence as the machine dipped toward the ground. In silence they saw it glide, steeply at first and then more gradually until its skids touched the earth to end its short and unspectacular flight. With wondering eyes they watched the mechanics race toward the stranded machine and Tissandier jump down to the field, annoyed and disappointed. Within minutes the men were wheeling the Wright biplane over the wet soggy ground back to its hangar to clear the field for others. Short though the flight had been, only a few hundred yards or so, Tissandier had, by this flight, inaugurated the Reims Flying Week and written aeronautical history.

By this time other machines were being assembled near the judges' box. Tissandier's flight was quickly followed by another Wright, and soon several aircraft were crossing the field to take advantage of the calmer conditions. One came down in a field of clover, but its descent was scarcely noted in the excitement.

Flying was more continuous now. There were several attempts on the "eliminating trials" for the Gordon Bennett Trophy and the other speed contests. Eugène Lefebvre in his French-made Wright took off for the Tour de Piste and quickly completed the single circuit of 10 kilometers in the excellent time of 8 minutes 58.8 seconds.

Before describing the races, the incidents, and the competitive events of the Reims meeting, some knowledge of the personalities involved is essential. These were the men who had designed and built the planes, the pilots who flew them, and the organizers responsible for solving the many problems that arose. It was these men who had planned with detailed care this milestone in aviation history, surmounting the difficulties with one objective: to focus the world's attention on the future possibilities of flying and its international benefits. There would be opposition, disappointments were certain, serious accidents could occur, pilots might be injured, some possibly killed, but these were exciting times and life was changing. Already, between Octave Chanute's first visit to France in 1903 and these August days of 1909 at Reims, France had experienced a growing interest in man's achievement in the air.

It had been only a few years earlier that the general public's attitude to flying had been one of indignant protestation. Ordinary men and women, gazing up to watch a balloon floating silently overhead, gave vent to their feelings. "If God had wanted us to fly, he would have given us wings." One wonders how they felt when several balloons slowly drifted across the sky in what was called a balloon race. No doubt it increased their critical opposition and religious resentment.

In 1884 an elongated cigar-shaped balloon called *La France,* driven by an 8½-horsepower electric motor, had been built for the French Army. By the turn of the century several more airships had been built, but they, like the nonmotorized balloons, were very much at the mercy of the weather. Balloons and airships, it was said, were only for fools and rich men.

One man who disagreed with these sentiments was Alberto Santos-Dumont, a rich Brazilian, who had first arrived in Paris in 1892. Five years later, still a young man of twenty-four, he was initiated into the excitement of ballooning and never lost his passion for aeronautics.

Relating his feelings after his first balloon flight in May 1897, Santos-Dumont wrote in his book *Dans l'Air* published in 1904: "Villages and woods, meadows and castles, pass below us like a moving picture from which the whistles of railway locomotives come sharply upwards. These, and the barking of dogs are the only sounds that penetrate the upper air around us. The human voice cannot pass upward into these boundless solitudes."

Santos-Dumont was destined to make the first real airplane flight in France in 1906.

It was a relatively insignificant incident in Australia, in 1895, that radically changed the world's mode of transportation and planted the "seed" for a new era. Lawrence Hargrave, a kite-flying devotee, was not satisfied with the conventional kites of Chinese or Persian origin, and persevered with a new idea of his own—the box kite. Hargrave made a frame of four wooden struts, which he partly covered with calico material. Using cross-struts for strength, he created a boxlike structure with the ends and middle open; to him it was a double kite. He tethered it to the ground with string, and soon, to the astonishment of doubtful onlookers, he had it soaring well above the ground. Hargrave changed the design several times until he was satisfied, yet made no attempt to fly it as a glider; to him it was just another kite.

But to others, Hargrave's contribution to flight was so

radically different from anything previously sent into the air that it quickly reached Europe and America. At first it was a novelty, but it soon found fertile soil in the Chicago office of a consulting engineer of international repute, Octave Chanute. Chanute, of French birth and parentage, had been brought to the United States as a boy but had retained his French connections. For some time he had been keenly interested in the gliding experiments of Otto Lilienthal in Germany and Percy Sinclair Pilcher in England, and had launched into a concentrated study of the German's exploits and the flight of birds which brought him into aerodynamics.

Chanute little thought of what would follow when he began his experiments in airfoils and active gliding over the sandhills near Lake Michigan in Indiana. Fascinated by Hargrave's kite, he built a larger one in which he could swing, partly between the upper framework and partly below. He used the double wing design, or biplane, one wing above the other, and soon made several gliding flights with varying success. Before long Chanute began a long sequence of correspondence with another flight enthusiast, Wilbur Wright, which continued until the Wrights were flying at Kitty Hawk. Chanute's collation of facts was a major influence on the brothers, helping them as they built their succession of gliders. His knowledge of flying soon placed Chanute in a most influential position during the world's rapidly burgeoning interest in flying.

Chanute's dominance was emphasized when, on a visit to his native France in April 1903 (and later, England), he lectured on aeronautics before the Aero Club of France. Chanute was determined to interest the airship-minded Aero Club in what he and the two Wrights had been doing in America, in their gliders and the visionary ideas of powered flight. He told the French flying enthusiasts what progress had been made in the heavier-than-air machines, how airships and balloons were soon to be relegated to a past era. His book *Progress in Flying Machines* had been published many years before, nine years, in fact, and now in person he could report on the incredible progress that had been made in the United States. He told how he had encouraged the Wright brothers and led them in their more scientific approach to the problem of flight, especially balance.

Chanute confounded the balloon- and airship-minded members of the French Aero Club, but only a few who listened were convinced of the practicability and wisdom of his lecture. While most of the scientists were skeptical of the progress which the Americans had made in gliding, Chanute won over two influential Frenchmen: Ernest Archdeacon, a financier, and Captain Ferdinand Ferber, an ardent balloonist in the French Balloon Corps. Both were active members of the French Aero Club and well known in French political and financial circles. Archdeacon, a lawyer, had been financially involved in the development of the French motorcar industry. To him, the heavier-than-air machine was the next step beyond the automobile. Did it not need a gasoline engine?

Archdeacon was emphatic in his condemnation of those Frenchmen who were still hesitant about the possibilities of the heavier-than-air machines and, only eight months before the Wright brothers flew their powered aircraft in North Carolina, told his fellow Aero Club members, "France does not hold the lead in the special science of aviation. Money is needed; put your hands in your pockets or we are beaten. The solution to flying is approaching very quickly."

Through Archdeacon's persuasion and influence, doors began to open. Cabinet ministers listened, the French Army took a new and keen interest, and now, in August 1909, through Archdeacon's convincing arguments, even the President of France himself had promised to be present at Reims. Ernest Archdeacon, for all his efforts in those very early days, could undoubtedly be called the father of French flying.

While Archdeacon financed and played politics, and Ferber experimented with his Chanute-type glider, Santos-Dumont, another member of the French Aero Club, was still more interested in airships than in either Chanute's or the Wright brothers' heavier-than-air machines. Early in 1904 he remarked to Archdeacon, "Chanute with all his gliding experiments can still only fly a few feet and always near the ground, whereas I can fly in my airships for miles and climb above the clouds. Can Chanute and his friends the Wrights equal this?" Santos-Dumont built five airships in the years after Chanute's visit to France.

Meanwhile, Archdeacon and Captain Ferber were collaborating in the design of a glider on the lines of the machine which the Wright brothers were flying in North Carolina. Although tethered by a long rope, the Archdeacon-Ferber glider lifted off the ground and gave them encouragement to continue further work on the project. Ferber was as enthusiastic as Archdeacon, and after many glider flights in the French Alps, he returned to Paris, keen to learn what the Wright brothers were doing in America.

Ferber's keenness urged him to go further, but other interests prevented him from flying full-time. Willing but unable for many reasons to take up active flying, Archdeacon needed someone to act as a pilot for him. Unfortunately, apart from Ferber, there was no one with flying experience. Archdeacon talked the problem over with Captain Ferber.

"We need someone with mechanical knowledge as well

as an inspired desire to fly," he commented. "We need someone who can repair a motorcar engine; sooner or later someone will put an engine into a glider and be free of the wind and independent of the weather which has plagued Santos-Dumont and his airships. Even Santos-Dumont has had to put an engine into his airships. What we need is a man who is not afraid of flying a glider and one who is useful with his hands. Someone who can train others. Do you know anyone?"

Ferber's response was to suggest the young man Gabriel Voisin. He was a good mechanic, even though he had been trained as an architect. He kept his own motorcar in first-class condition, and what was more, he was extraordinarily keen on flying.

Archdeacon frowned as he nodded. "I remember that young man. He talked a lot about flying a kite, but nothing else. I did not know he had a motorcar. Send him round again and I will talk to him. Maybe he will be the man we are looking for."

When Voisin was still a teen-ager, he and his brother Charles had rebuilt a steam engine using pieces of pipe, old valves, and other fittings, which they had found in the engineering yard where the disused and emasculated steam engine had been dumped. The brothers fitted it into a boat and raised enough steam to drive a propeller.

A few years later Voisin's first automobile was a gasoline-driven tricycle. After he had been shown how to use it, he drove it away and quickly found his brother Charles.

"How does it work?" Charles asked.

"I don't know, but we'll take it apart and soon find out." Gabriel's reply was indicative of his perpetual curiosity. With the aid of a screwdriver, pliers, and a few more essential tools, the brothers dismantled the engine and studied it. It was only a beginning.

Motorcars, then in their infancy, were strange-looking contraptions. Many were three-wheeled affairs—a tricycle with a 2- or 3-horsepower motor. Voisin was one of the first Frenchmen to actually make one of his own. With the help of his brother the motorcar was built with solid tires and a lack of shock absorbers; they had to make their own piston rings, a gear wheel, and the other parts that proved necessary. In this motorcar Gabriel Voisin drove three hundred miles to Neuville-sur-Saône, near Lyons, arriving there stiff with cold and his body numb from the hard seat on which he had to sit. It took him six days to reach Neuville—fifty miles a day—with many hours spent daily replacing broken or damaged parts. Voisin's knowledge of the internal combustion engine was gained through bitter experience. When others challenged this knowledge, and they did, he could and did vehemently resent their imputations with annoyance.

As with his later airplane designs, Gabriel was always ready to add innovations. To his tricycle he added a modified garden wheelbarrow. Charles could accompany him now, a useful companion, especially when the car kept stopping and needed repairs. It was not long before Gabriel's tricycle could travel, carrying Charles and their mother in the attached trailer, at a fairly regular speed of 12 miles an hour.

Then came the fascination of Lawrence Hargrave's box kite. Always eager to create something worthwhile, Gabriel and his younger brother had been intrigued by a magazine article that illustrated Hargrave's new idea for a kite. It was not long before Gabriel's creative brain enabled them to improve on Hargrave's construction, and he and his brother were flying their own interpretation of the box kite on a nearby field. Their success was due to an unforeseen incident. While they were trying to get the box kite into the air, and having great difficulty in doing so, they were caught in a sudden storm. The rain soaked the canvas, binding the wooden struts and curving the surfaces. The effect was remarkable. To their astonishment the rain-soaked kite was now hard to hold; it lifted Gabriel off his feet as he struggled to retain a hold on the tethering rope in the gusty wind that followed. Even when assisted by Charles, the two brothers had difficulty in getting the big kite back on the ground.

It was not until some days later that the true significance of what this meant was brought home to them. Once again they decided to fly the kite in the same field near their home. It was a beautiful warm morning, the sun was shining, a little wind was blowing, a warm breeze that was ideal, but their kite failed to rise more than a few feet before it flopped back on the ground. They tried again and again but without success. Charles looked at the fallen kite and scratched his head.

"Remember how it lifted in that storm the other day!" he exclaimed. "We couldn't do much when it was dry, but when it was soaked we had a job to hold it down. Let's soak it now and see what happens."

Charles ran to a stream at the other end of the field and brought back a can of water which he poured onto the dry canvas. They soaked the kite and tried once again to get it into the upper air. The effect was now instantaneous. As the box-kite fabric shrunk, the struts were again twisted and the lifting power returned with the same force as before. They put it down to the bending of the calico-covered wings, or plane surfaces, which could only occur when the kite was wet. By moving the tethering line forward or backward they found they could control the kite's upward or downward movements. Time and time again, when the wind was blowing hard, Gabriel Voisin was lifted off his feet and into the air. Once he was a good two or three feet above the ground he could control the kite's movements. It was great fun for the boys, but nothing more; the next day they put their kite away for other and more important interests and kite flying was forgotten. At the age of twenty Gabriel Voisin began his studies at the Architectural Section of the École des Beaux Arts in Paris.

French flying really began when Gabriel Voisin, who had met Ferber after hearing the latter give a lecture on gliding in Lyons (he had been describing Chanute's glider and the Wrights' experiments in 1903), abandoned his dull existence as an architectural student for the more exciting life of flying. Unknown in 1904, this was the man who in the few years ahead was to be a dominating figure in aeronautics, teaching and helping others, and ultimately to become one of the world's leading aircraft manufacturers.

Voisin told of what happened on the fateful morning when he visited Archdeacon for a second time: "Archdeacon told me of the troubles he had been having with the carburetor of his Renault car. I had the good fortune to find the trouble within minutes and make the carburetor function satisfactorily. Next day, without further discussion, Archdeacon agreed to my flying his glider and to form a company with sufficient finances."

So, from that moment, flying became Gabriel Voisin's life work. It took him to Reims and, later, into World War I as one of France's leading aircraft manufacturers known internationally as Voisin Frères.

His first trial took place in Paris when he was only twenty-five. The Seine, flowing slowly through the heart of the French capital, has, over the centuries, seen some strange sights but none stranger than the events of that early morning of June 6, 1905. The mist was clearing to reveal a small group of workmen busily engaged in attaching sections of white fabric-covered frames to two elongated floats resting on the grass alongside the river. The sun was well above the trees before the finished assembly was moved slowly toward the water. It looked like a huge white bird as it slid gracefully down the grassy bank. Once in the water it was tied to a small boat while the workmen scrambled back to a more secure position. Above them a gentle breeze swayed the poplars, their leaves soughing and sighing as if in sympathy with the anxious men looking at their handiwork—the Archdeacon-Ferber glider that Voisin had built. Slowly and carefully Voisin stepped onto one of the floats and pulled himself into the pilot's seat.

It was past noon before the glider was pulled into midstream by a small rowing boat and the towrope quickly thrown to the towing launch which had been slowly following the others. In the stern were two anxious-looking men, one controlling the powerful racing boat as it chugged quietly into the current and one who held the helm with the ease of an expert helmsman. This was Monsieur Tellier, the owner of the towing boat with its 150-horsepower engine. The other man who had just caught the towline and was deftly securing it was Ernest Archdeacon.

Once in the glider, Voisin settled down to handle the controls. The group of onlookers had grown into a large crowd, with the police as keen as the rest to see what was happening. The assembled Parisians filled the bridge and in their excitement were trying to get down to the path by the river's edge. A sign from Voisin to Archdeacon was passed to Tellier, the boat moved forward, and the towline tightened as it lifted out of the water. Slowly and cautiously Tellier moved the launch away from the Billancourt Bridge, the glider following smoothly. He increased its speed, and in seconds the racing boat was rushing toward the Pont Sèvres Bridge in the distance, Voisin firmly holding the controls.

Moments later the swaying glider started to rise. Soon it was clear of the surface, well above the river, guided by the skillful Voisin. The controls were working perfectly; the glider, like a graceful bird, was now in steady flight.

Captain Ferber, stopwatch in hand, ran along the water's edge, excited and out of breath. Voisin was the least perturbed; too occupied with the controls to keep the glider on an even keel, watching the launch below and the bridge ahead, he was quite unmoved. At last the launch slowed to a stop, and with the ease of a gull alighting on the water Voisin brought his machine down with hardly a splash. No flight could have been more successful.

"It was easy," he called to Archdeacon across the gap of disturbed, foam-covered water. "The controls were perfect. She flies like a bird. No trouble at all. I'd like to try it over land—towing it with a motorcar. She came down easily, too—no worries at all."

The police were holding back the crowds that had been attracted to the river. Only a small group of officials were allowed down by the water's edge where the glider floated. Voisin climbed out of the control seat and jumped to the ground. Ferber reached them as Archdeacon joined the group of excited officials, newspaper reporters, and photographers. One of the most interested men waiting by the towed plane was a black-moustached smiling Frenchman. He made no effort to converse—Louis Blériot until then had only been interested in motorcars. Ferber and Archdeacon were surrounded by a crowd of gesticulating photographers. What Blériot had to say would keep for later, but he, too, was being infected by the bug of flying. Flying was more exciting than motorcar racing, and he had the money to make it possible.

Once back in the Syndicat d'Aviation's works near Boulogne-Billancourt, the days passed quickly for Voisin. There was much activity, and Archdeacon left him very much alone. Blériot was an early caller; he wanted Voisin to build a glider for him and he had plenty of ideas, even suggesting that they should go into partnership. With Blériot there were no half measures: he had the money and was willing to spend it. Voisin always needed money and Blériot's was as good as the next man's, so he listened with interest.

Two months after the successful Seine flight, Voisin appeared again at the same spot, but this time his two backers, Archdeacon and Ferber, were showing considerably more interest. Louis Blériot was there, too, with a glider that Voisin had made.

This time there was another and differently powered racing boat and helmsman to tow the gliders into the air. Instead of the patient, cautious Tellier and his Panhard-driven launch, they had Léon Levavasseur, a smiling bearded man with a dark cloth-type yachtsman's cap. He was using one of his fastest Antoinette boats, but unfortunately towing was something new to Levavasseur. He knew a lot about engines but little about handling a boat, especially when it was roped to a fragile glider.

The success of the trial two months earlier was not repeated. The Archdeacon glider which before had flown seven-hundred feet at treetop level was now to be towed by a newcomer to flying, whose inexperience was soon apparent. When the signal was given, the towline suddenly jerked taut, and off went Levavasseur in his speeding motorboat. The suddenness of the start confused Voisin, who tried to control the swerving glider as it began to rise above the water. Its swaying wings dipped, first to one side and then the other, like a kite being pulled too swiftly in a gale. Luckily for Voisin, Levavasseur's engine stopped as sud-

denly as it started, leaving the glider to flop back ignominiously onto the water.

Blériot's machine was tried next, but this was even more
of a failure. Due to inexperienced power boat control and
towing, Blériot's Voisin-made glider began to swing from
side to side. It half rose, swung again, and as one wing
dipped, it struck the river surface and collapsed in a terrific
crash. The next moment Gabriel Voisin, still at the controls,
disappeared beneath a pile of debris comprised of broken
struts, severed and coiling wires, and torn canvas. With
difficulty they pulled Voisin ashore. The blame lay fairly
and squarely on the bad, almost mad handling of the towline. It was Voisin's last glide on the Seine. He preferred the
fields around his factory, and when Blériot came to see him
the following day, fully understanding the reason for the
failure, a closer financial association was amicably arranged.

Thus the pattern of Voisin's career in aeronautics was to
change more than once in the months and years that followed. Between the days of the Seine trials and the races at
Reims were four years of trials and troubles with enough
successes to make life worthwhile. He taught many men to
fly, helped many more in their careers, but he had his
tragic moments. His brother Charles was killed in a car
accident, other airplane makers came to the top—some to
surpass him temporarily—but his years of experience, his
wide knowledge of all the facets of airplane design, stood
him in good stead. His prestige was high when he entered
into the Reims Flying Week.

During these years, Archdeacon had another close friend
besides Captain Ferber, one whose services he could co-opt
when necessary, and one of the wealthiest men in France,
the oil industrialist Henri Deutsch de la Meurthe. Deutsch,
as he was known, came of a highly influential Jewish family.
He was a well-known sportsman, a friend of struggling

JEFFERSON - MADISON REGIONAL
LIBRARY   CHARLOTTESVILLE, VA.

artists, especially musicians, but his chief interest and one
which brought him into flying was the gasoline engine and,
with it, petroleum products. Deutsch was generous when it
came to motorcars, often giving a car to anyone he liked
or who had helped him or had subscribed to his charities.

It was Deutsch who first thought of offering prize money
to encourage fliers. He had offered 50,000 francs for the
first man to fly an airship to Paris from the French Aero
Club's flying field at Chalais Meudon to Paris, around the
Eiffel Tower, and back. Previously, in 1903, following
Chanute's visit to Paris, Deutsch had offered 25,000 francs
to the first pilot to fly a heavier-than-air machine 25 meters
(82 feet). Archdeacon, not to be outdone by his friend,
added an equal amount, and it became known as the
Deutsch-Archdeacon prize, the first prize to be given to encourage "powered flight."

These prizes and others which generously-minded
wealthy Frenchmen gave to further the cause of aviation,
when flying was in its infancy, encouraged ambitious aircraft pioneers to fly farther, faster, higher, and with greater
control. Mayors of cities vied with each other, offering cash
prizes for flights to or in their cities, to gain publicity for
their regions. It was these early attempts to attract fliers that
in August 1909, through the influence of the French Aero
Club led by Ernest Archdeacon, the mayor of Reims was
encouraged to sponsor that first great air attraction. To
make its success assured, the mayor of Reims also persuaded the big champagne growers to provide the valuable
cash prizes.

Throughout the critical years Archdeacon and Deutsch
were popularizing the idea of flight, Captain Ferber's enthusiasm had not waned. With his military connections, he
transferred his affections from balloons to gliders. Before
Reims was being planned he had become a pilot and was

soon playing a leading part in getting the Wright brothers established in France. It was due to Ferber's efforts that the groundwork was laid to sell the Wright patents in France. Their wing warping system and their knowledge of aeronautics were vital to airplane manufacture, and Ferber's action gave French flying much needed help.

Today the names of Ernest Archdeacon, Henri Deutsch de la Meurthe, and Captain Ferdinand Ferber are forgotten except by a few, but it was on the foundation of their work that European aviation was built. Archdeacon was mainly responsible not only for the Reims Flying Week but, with his genius for organizing and his indefatigable energy, for its success. With Captain Ferber he persuaded the senior generals of the French Army to attend, and they, in turn, brought their counterparts from Great Britain. Following this, Archdeacon, aided by Deutsch de la Meurthe, crowned his efforts by ensuring the presence of the President of France, Armand Fallières.

Captain Ferber flew at Reims in a Voisin biplane under the assumed name of F. de Rue. On the opening day, under the worst conditions, he failed to get off the ground, but that did not abate his enthusiasm. It is tragic to note that he was killed in an air crash not many weeks after the Reims meeting, for there were not many men who worked harder for French aeronautics than Ferdinand Ferber. He had hoped the meeting would be more international, but this did not detract from its success. In spite of the bad weather at the beginning of the week, Reims became a national event and one that had a stupendous effect on the entire world. In those early years before World War I, Reims became synonymous with competitive flying.

The First Day

In spite of the early rain and strong winds, the weather on the opening day cleared, and by early afternoon the spectators at the Reims-Bétheny racetrack were well rewarded for their optimism. The grandstands and the standing areas were filled, with a few of the more daring fans climbing the barriers. They stood by the doorways of the long line of hangars to gain shelter from the wind, hoping to catch a glimpse of their favorite pilot or airplane builder or to get a closer view of the strange-looking fabric-covered machines inside. Hundreds, perhaps thousands, were standing in the fields bordering the racetrack, waiting patiently, if only to see the planes fly overhead or skim across the surrounding fields. Like actors in a drama, the great airmen, whose names were becoming household words, were gathering in the hangars as they waited for flying to be declared possible.

The first event scheduled for the opening day would decide who would represent France for the Gordon Bennett Trophy. There were twenty entries, and the pilots, despite the bad weather, had already drawn lots for the starting order. After Esnault-Pelterie had failed to get off the ground and Tissandier's short flight had ended in engine failure, other machines were brought from the hangars. As flying conditions slowly improved, the area around the judges' box saw increased activity. Every machine had its team of helpers as it was wheeled out of its hangar, and though these were mostly mechanics, there was no dearth of men anxious to assist in bringing any plane onto the field. Some machines were pulled into position on a low trolley; others were towed by a horse, to the amusement of the onlookers. While they were waiting, new signal flags fluttered to the top of the flagstaff: Louis Blériot was about to fly, and the announcement rapidly spread through the crowd. Blériot's popularity was unbounded. Every newspaper had shown his photograph—a smiling handsome man whom every woman adored. Had he not flown la Manche (the English Channel) with his legs burned and partly crippled? A cheer of delight rose, increasing to a roar, as Blériot's monoplane rose from the ground and began to circle the field, dipping slightly in front of the main stand in a triumphant flight. The audience was thrilled, cheering whenever Blériot passed overhead and waving their hats until he glided back to the judges' box.

Hubert Latham, who only a few weeks before had been beaten by Blériot for the cross-Channel prize, followed the older man. His plane number was 13, but the ominous number did not deter him, and he managed to fly about five hundred yards before his engine began to misfire. The crowd was not surprised as it spluttered, started again, then stopped altogether; the people were getting used to this. Their groans of disappointment were all part of the fun, and they were glad to see Latham glide back safely to earth without crashing.

The next pilot in the air was Eugène Lefebvre, in a

Wright biplane. Almost unknown to the general public and a comparative newcomer to flying circles, Lefebvre soon had everyone on his feet. After a quick takeoff in front of the grandstands, he continued without stopping, completing circuit after circuit until he had flown for more than twenty minutes. His flying was performed with an ease that was more spectacular than the veteran Blériot's. He put the Wright plane into steep banks, dipping swiftly and rising with startling suddenness, demonstrating how easy it was to fly and giving the onlookers the thrill they had been waiting for. The Reims Flying Meeting was at last becoming something real and exciting.

The wind was getting stronger now, and gusts were harassing the pilots. Some, like Captain Ferber, could not get off the ground or would not risk rising more than a few feet before returning to the soggy earth. Their machines were still comparatively frail, a wooden framework with wings of strong cotton canvas or sailcloth, doped to make it taut and smooth to the onrushing air. To add to the structural strength the wings were braced with cross-wires between the struts of the upper and lower planes. Monoplanes, too, had bracing wires, which stretched from the wing tips to one or two vertical struts on each side of the pilot's seat. Planes varied in size, shape, and weight; the Wright and Farman machines, the largest of those competing at Reims, weighed over 1,200 pounds.

The contest for the choice of the three French champions to compete for the Gordon Bennett Cup ended that morning in a farce. Not one of the many competitors could stay in flight for more than a few minutes. The official distance to be flown was 20 kilometers, almost 12½ miles, but this, in a gusty crosswind, seemed an impossibility. It was too dangerous even for the sturdiest machine.

After lunch more people, encouraged by a little sunshine

and patches of blue sky, arrived from nearby Reims, but
they were greeted by the news that the Gordon Bennett
Trophy might have to be abandoned if the wind continued.
The rain started again, and with gusts of wind sometimes as
high as thirty miles an hour, no more flying seemed possible.
Since no one had bettered Lefebvre's and Blériot's performances, these two were selected as the first French representa-
tives for the race. They would compete against Glenn
Curtiss at the end of the week. Since the organizers needed
a third it was finally decided to add Hubert Latham to the
French team.

Later in the afternoon the weather improved again. The
storm ended as suddenly as it had begun, and activity began again in and around the hangars.

When flying restarted, Tissandier was again successful.
This time his Wright biplane stayed in the air for some
time. He was joined by Louis Paulhan in his Voisin biplane
and then by several Farman biplanes until the spectators
were given an unexpected thrill when they saw seven planes
in the air at the same time. It was a wonderful sight, and
David Lloyd George, the British Cabinet minister and official representative, was so fascinated by what he saw during that early Sunday evening that he commented with
typical Welsh rhetorical speech, after several Wright biplanes passed before the stands in close company, "It
seems to me the Wright machines are writing history on the
clouds."

If this was a little exaggerated, it was nevertheless true to
say that the Wright biplanes were giving a great exhibition
of their speed and reliability. But they were not alone, for
Sommer, in his Farman, gave a surprising demonstration of
intermittent flying until he finally came down after being in
the air for almost 1 hour and 20 minutes. His flight was
not continuous, but he demonstrated how easy it was to

land and take off continuously with only short periods on the ground.

Other planes were being flown with equal confidence: Paulhan, competing for the Prix de la Vitesse speed prize, flew the 30 kilometers in 32 minutes 50 seconds—an average speed of 35 miles an hour. While this was not good enough to impress those who wanted speed, it satisfied the majority, who were content with just seeing a plane in the air.

Before the day ended, five aviators—Tissandier, Comte Charles de Lambert, Lefebvre, Paulhan, and Sommer— succeeded in covering the 30 kilometers for this same speed prize, the Prix de la Vitesse, the three Wright machines taking the first three places. The results of the first day of this event were so close that Tissandier, who was first, and Lefebvre and De Lambert, who were both bracketed second, were only 1.6 seconds apart. Latham in his Antoinette and Cockburn in his Farman also flew that afternoon.

These flights gave the pilots many opportunities to show off their skill and to thrill the spectators with hair-raising stunts. As one machine would come down, another would quickly take its place. Some would swoop around the grandstands, often climbing steeply, while another dived to a few feet above the ground. Early in the afternoon the audience had seen Tissandier passing over the slower Etienne Bunau-Varilla. Blériot caused considerable excitement when, overshooting his landing, he charged into a pile of wheat sheaves, scattering the bundles in all directions and breaking his propeller. In all, the first day's flying represented a total of over three hundred kilometers by all the "birdmen" in their many flights.

The rules for the meeting had been carefully prepared. As there would be many competitions during the week involving numerous qualifying laps, a competitor had to declare which event he was going for, and naturally his performance stood only for that particular event. To enable those present to know which event was being flown and by whom, a simple arrangement of signal flags was used. One set of indicating flags would be flown at the top of the pylon flagstaff near the judges' box and another near the grandstands. The flags were of different shapes and colors and told which competitor was flying and for which event. It also gave the spectators such other information as whether a record had been made, whether a landing was made successfully within the rules, and weather conditions. In a horse race or even an automobile race, all the contestants could be lined up at the start of the race and it would be easy for a crowd to follow the race and know immediately who was the winner—but not so with flying. To get over this problem, the organizers devised their ingenious but simple code so that everyone would know what was happening. It was a success and satisfied everyone.

For instance, a white disk with a white rectangle and another white disk all flying together meant that the plane on the ground would not take off due to engine trouble, and if a red triangle replaced the second white disk, the spectators would know that the plane had suffered some damage. The changing of a propeller would be indicated by a white disk, a white rectangle, and a red rectangle. Arrivals of VIPs were also announced by signal flags. Should a head of state or a very senior minister or foreign diplomat arrive, he would be welcomed by the flags. Signals were also used for internal use, if a mechanic was needed in a hurry or if a pilot had made a wrong turn when rounding the judges' "corner tower" and so on.

Contestants were restricted at all times to the event they had "declared." If Blériot had declared for the 30 kilometers or three-lap speed race, the Prix de la Vitesse, he

could not apply the fastest lap of 10 kilometers to the Prix
de Tour de Piste, or take the two fastest laps for the Gordon
Bennett Trophy. Each event had its own day—as directed
by the judges.

These arrangements were planned by the organizers to
help the competitors meet the vagaries of the weather and
prevent arguments occurring later. It enabled those competing to get their planes in readiness without too much official
interference. These were early days of flying, and many
things could happen. An accident one day could delay a
flier trying to repair his plane in time for a scheduled event.
The Gordon Bennett Trophy was timed to take place on
Saturday, August 28, to draw as many people as possible
to the Bétheny racetrack. It also left the next day available
in case the weather was too bad for flying on Saturday.

The course at Bétheny—it was always referred to as the
Reims meeting—was a flat ellipse of 10 kilometers, 6.2
miles, when measured around the marking pylons. The long
side of the course parallel to the grandstands was 3,750
meters, above 2⅓ miles. The shorter distance at each end
of the course was a little more than ¾ mile between the
markers. The only disadvantage was that of trying to keep
a machine in view from the stands when it was at the far
end of the course. Field glasses were expensive, and not
many had thought of bringing them. Those fortunate
enough to have them, however, could enjoy the distant flying, but the majority, who lacked this aid, had to be content
with what they could see nearby. Still, there was plenty to
see, including the activity of the ground staffs, the mechanics pulling a plane onto the field, and the machine
taking off alongside the stands.

There would be seven events, or competitive races, as
the general public called them. The most valuable event
would be the Grand Prix de la Champagne et de la Ville

de Reims for 100,000 francs—$20,000—worth 50,000 francs to the winner and prize money for the next five. There would be eliminating trials on the opening day, but the final awards would not be announced until the last day.

The most spectacular race was to be the Coupe Gordon Bennett, given by the publisher of the New York *Herald*. The magnificent solid silver trophy with 50,000 francs added ($10,000) was, in those days, not a small prize. What was more important was the prestige and fame it gave to the winner. It was the world's first international speed race—the fastest of two circuits, of 10 kilometers each. Speed always captures the imagination, and this promised to be no exception. Reims, famous for champagne, was now gathering worldwide fame for flying. The Reims meeting marked an epoch in the age of flight—the beginning of an era. Man's attitude was changing from scoffing to a piquancy of optimistic realization.

The next most valuable prize would also be a test of speed, the Prix de la Vitesse. It would be flown over three circuits for a total of 30 kilometers. The winner would take 10,000 francs ($2,000 dollars), the second 5,000 francs, out of a total prize of 20,000 francs, with the remainder to the third and fourth.

The other speed prize, called the Prix de Tour de Piste, or "around the track," would be, as its name indicated, one lap of 10 kilometers and worth 7,000 francs to the winner and 3,000 francs to the second. It was expected to be a race among Curtiss, Blériot, and Farman, with Blériot the favorite.

To add to the general interest of the meeting and to give it attractions more than just speed, there were less spectacular events such as the altitude prize for 10,000 francs and a prize for carrying passengers 10 kilometers. Henri Farman was planning to carry two passengers, an unheard-of feat in those days. To add to the novelty of the week and to give the spectators a final glimpse of the fading era of airships, the meeting included a Prix des Aeronauts. Two dirigibles would compete, the *Colonel Renard* and the *Zodiac,* and would be timed over a distance of 50 kilometers, about 31 miles.

The engines on which so much depended at Reims varied in size and design from the 3-cylinder Anzani, rated at 35/40 horsepower, to the 55-horsepower 8-cylinder Renault and the 50-horsepower Antoinette, also with 8 cylinders. These were stationary, but recently a new engine had been introduced to flying—a rotary engine called the Gnome. It was an air-cooled rotary unit of 7 cylinders, with the propeller and engine bolted together and revolving as one.

Great credit must be given to the organizers who were responsible for planning and judging the races. It was not easy to maintain a calm atmosphere, solving the many problems that were bound to occur with so many different personalities present. Arguments would quickly overstep the bounds of reason, and quarrels and wrangling could not be avoided, but no major incident involving serious trouble was reported. There was a feeling of camaraderie between the officials and participants. It was quite apparent that the future of the air industry lay in the hands of the competitors. Differences were forgotten in the one desire to give the world a view of what progress had been made in the art of flying and what it could look for in the future.

The organizers were treading on unknown ground. No such flying meeting had ever been held before. It could be a fiasco or a dramatic success; it could even make France the world aviation leader. All that was needed was fair weather and co-operation combined with the fighting spirit of those taking part.

While there was no doubt that the money prizes attracted entries, there were other reasons. Apart from prestige, it gave the aircraft designers and builders experience in flying under adverse conditions. They gained knowledge in competition. This was an industry where there was no scientific backbone of research and development; knowledge was gained by trial and error. They were groping in the dark, copying, imitating, devising, with little knowledge of competitive flying. It encouraged some of the lesser known men, who, like Louis Bréguet, were destined to play an important role in the first air war to be fought five years later.

Of the more noted world fliers the Wrights' absence was disappointing, particularly since Orville was in Germany at this time. Wilbur, negotiating with the United States Government for the sale of Wright planes, maintained it was up to the French licensees to supervise the French-built Wright planes taking part; everyone from Archdeacon down regretted their action.

The other absentee of note was the wealthy, volatile, eccentric, and unpredictable Alberto Santos-Dumont. Here was an ardent enthusiast of flying; he had been flying dirigibles when the Wright brothers were learning to glide and before they flew their first powered biplane at Kitty Hawk. He had designed and built his first powered plane in 1906 at Bagatelle, a district of Paris. He had done more for French aviation than many who were flying at Reims, yet this wealthy enigmatic Brazilian preferred to stay at St. Cyr, near Paris, only a hundred miles away, saying he was not interested in prizes.

There were other non-French absentees, the better known pilots like the Anglo-American Colonel Samuel Franklin Cody, Elicottero Ellehammer from Copenhagen, and Horatio Barber, Alliott Verdon Roe, and Robert Blackburn—

an English trio who were already building and flying planes of their own design.

It was natural then for the French public to be only interested in those who took an active part in the flying—the pilots they saw in the air whose names made daily news. As the first decade of the twentieth century progressed, France was fortunate to have many wealthy men who were keen on helping the aeronautical industry. In other countries, the United States included, the wealthy financiers were skeptical, even afraid. Balloons and airships were only for the frivolous who could spend thousands of dollars for the thrill of floating above the earth. But in France, with the coming of the heavier-than-air machine, men like Santos-Dumont, Archdeacon, Léon Delagrange, Henri Deutsch de la Meurthe, Ferber, and others of the Aero Club of France had progressive ideas and quickly turned their attention and their money to this new thrill. It should be remembered, too, that in 1907 there were only about nine recognized pilots in Europe, men who had actually flown heavier-than-air machines. They were Santos-Dumont, the first to make an officially witnessed flight in Europe; Trajan Vuia, an Austrian Parisian; the Englishman Horatio Phillips; Gabriel Voisin; Blériot; Esnault-Pelterie; Delagrange; Alfred de Pischof; and, of course, Henri Farman. This is the order in which they successfully piloted a powered aircraft, between 1906 and 1907. Undoubtedly it was Voisin's experience in construction and Farman's flair for designing mechanical equipment that gave them the lead in aeronautics during those years.

Twenty-eight pilots had entered into the various events at Reims. And when the first day of racing ended, they had only managed to whet the appetite of their audience.

The Second Day

Monday's dawn brought a calm bright morning, the weather having changed overnight. The rain and blustering winds of the previous day had gone, and as the sun rose, the Reims racecourse became the scene of intense activity. For the flying man it could not have been better. A slight breeze fanned the ground to greet the early arrivals and bring hope to the few who had stayed overnight in the hangars, working and sleeping near their machines; already they were preparing to bring their planes into the open for another day's flying.

The peace of the countryside was broken early when Blériot, always an active flier who awoke with the dawn, climbed into the seat of his monoplane. He threw the control stick from left to right, then backward and forward, as if to loosen it before flying. He looked at the waiting men, paused for a moment to make sure all was well, then called to his chief mechanic, who was already holding the propeller, to swing. With the engine soon running at full speed it took all four of his mechanics to keep the tail down. This was a crucial moment for Blériot, but he was satisfied. Waving the mechanics away, he moved the plane slowly toward the pylon. It was six o'clock, and the only onlookers were a few of the track staff, some policemen and mechanics; it was too early for the general public.

With effortless ease the plane rose into the air. It lifted easily, and Blériot was content to keep it only a few feet above the ground. He banked carefully around the "marker" post and returned again to where his mechanics were waiting anxiously. He dropped steadily, gliding smoothly to a standstill. He was satisfied with his trial. Now that his monoplane was flying well, Blériot was at last ready for the speed trials which were scheduled later. After the crew had wheeled the plane away, several other pilots, not to be outdone, were soon on the field with their machines. The time was passing quickly, and many were still flying when the first spectators arrived to take up their places in the grandstand.

Soon after breakfast several Farman planes were up, with the Voisins and Wrights adding to the display. They circled, with two and sometimes three in the air simultaneously. There was a thrill of excitement as they passed overhead. The interest increased as a speck in the distant sky developed into a long cigar-shaped dirigible—the *Colonel Renard,* piloted by Henry Kapferer. High above the darting, circling heavier-than-air machines, it sailed gracefully around the field giving an air of superiority in its slower movement. In contrast with the noisier planes the *Colonel Renard* floated majestically and gracefully. It had come from Meaux, an hour and a half away. The *Renard* was due to compete with other airships for the Prix des Aeronauts to be flown later in the week.

The morning ended with Louis Paulhan making several circuits of the course to test his plane for the long-distance

event he was keen to win. But after lunch, when the expect-
ant hopes of the crowd were raised for more active and
competitive flying, the wind returned and for some time the
gusty conditions kept all the planes grounded. It gave the
occupants of the stands an opportunity to walk around and
exchange news with their friends and discuss the morning's
flying. Many dined at tables in front of the buffet stand,
while they greeted their friends.

It was an odd setting for Parisian society. The white
tablecloths flapping in the wind, waiters hurrying to and
from the tables with champagne corks popping significantly.
Very little wine was drunk that week—at least by the
wealthier visitors. Was this not the champagne country?
Were not the champagne producers sponsoring the meeting? Their poorer countrymen might have brought *vin
ordinaire* with their picinic baskets of meager loaves of
bread and country cheese, but for the elite—and there were
many hundreds at Reims that day—lunch was taken at the
tables, an occasion to see and be seen. After the limited
space for dining tables on the ground was occupied, the
rich visitors would dine in the buffet stand amid the noisy
clatter of plates and cutlery and the constant hum of conversation.

After lunch the wind was still somewhat gusty when one
or two planes ventured into the air. For Bunau-Varilla it
was not one of his happier days. After taking off, his plane
was caught in the cross currents and blown crab-wise away
from the course. He desperately tried to regain control but
without success. Realizing his limited power, he dropped
suddenly and, unable to get back to the flying field, found
himself in a field of oats much to the annoyance of a surprised farmer. With gesticulations and vehement declara-
tions of reprisals, Bunau-Varilla had to withdraw ignominiously before the farmer was satisfactorily pacified.

Not long after Bunau-Varilla landed among the ripening oats, Henri Fournier took off for a preliminary circuit before qualifying for the Grand Prix. But some bad timing or error of judgment marred his takeoff. It was typical of what could happen in those early days of visual signals before radiotelephones were invented. His takeoff was slow, and his machine crossed the official starting line before it was airborne. Fournier, unaware that he had not adhered to the rules, continued flying. It was only when he approached the starting post for the second time that he saw the signal that told him of his mistake in starting, meaning his first circuit had been in vain.

This upset Fournier and his Gallic temper rose. Vexed and obviously upset, he swung the plane round as if to land once again by the hangars. His action, taken suddenly without care, was clumsy and incompetent. One wing shot upward, the other dropped, and with the plane flying only a few feet above the ground, it touched down, bringing Fournier to earth in a noisy crash that brought mechanics and gendarmes running toward the spot. The wing crumbled beneath the undercarriage, leaving the fuselage and tail plane leaning to one side as Fournier clambered from his seat onto the ground. Although not a serious crash, it prevented Fournier from flying his Voisin anymore that day.

With the wind dying down and better conditions prevailing toward four o'clock, there was renewed activity around the hangars. Lefebvre was the first to get into the air. Without any "aerobatics," as it was later called, he concentrated on careful flying over the circular course which represented 10 kilometers. He banked steeply but kept well above the ground, determined not to repeat Fournier's earlier mishap. After two circuits of fast flying, he covered 21¼ kilometers in 20 minutes 14.4 seconds, about 33¼ miles an hour, not a very fast time even in those days.

While Lefebvre was flying, Paulhan followed into the air and stayed for some time. This was Paulhan's first attempt on the Grand Prix de la Champagne, and he tested his Voisin biplane not only for speed but for endurance. Cross-country flights were not common in 1909; they were risky, aerial maps were unknown, and it was quite an adventure to fly over what was, from their viewpoint, unexplored country. Landmarks that could be distinguished from the ground were strangely different when seen from the air. Fields and woods were divided by roads. There were no wide highways as we know them today. Some roads were little more than cart tracks where automobiles dare not go. Towns were distinguished from villages only by their size. Churches seemed to be lost in their gray slated roofs. The only safe guides were the railway tracks, but even these were of doubtful assistance where junctions divided the lines. It took the most daring pilots to try a cross-country flight and then only with good flying conditions and never too early in the morning when ground mists obscured the countryside. So it was safer to stay within sight of the Bétheny area even if it meant continuous circling of the short 10-kilometer course.

One of the earliest of the cross-country fliers was Louis Paulhan. In the years following Reims, Paulhan pioneered this progressive side of aviation making a name for himself and winning many valuable money prizes in Europe and the United States. It was not therefore surprising that at Reims in 1909 Paulhan concentrated on the endurance long-flying events in preference to the speed races. On this Monday afternoon he flew with a consistency that kept the onlookers enthused as he passed and repassed the grandstands without mishap or engine trouble. After almost an hour's flying, the longest by far that day, he easily qualified for the Grand Prix. His flight of 56 kilometers was clocked at 58 minutes 48.8 seconds—an average speed of almost 34 miles an hour.

Blériot, who had started the day's flying long before the public began to arrive, decided to go up again. He was flying a new monoplane which he called his No. XII, a more elegant design than the old XI. It was higher and more streamlined in appearance. It was a two-seater monoplane, the first of its kind. Hitherto passengers were carried out of courtesy and seldom in a monoplane with its limited space. Blériot had designed his XII for speed, with the Gordon Bennett Race as his objective. "Power and speed go together," he declared, and for this race he had installed a 50-horsepower E.N.V. engine instead of the 25- and 40-horsepower 3-cylinder Anzani engines he had used in his earlier planes. The Wrights and Farmans had used 4- and 5-cylinder engines until Levavasseur introduced his Antoinette engine of 8 cylinders like the new Renault, so Blériot decided to use the larger E.N.V., which was a British engine, and while rated at 50 horsepower Blériot hoped it would give him the speed he needed to beat Curtiss. With pride he called it the *White Eagle,* and he set great hopes on this, his fastest plane. It had only one fault, bad directional control, but something had to be sacrificed for speed if he was to win the Gordon Bennett Trophy. He had another in reserve, his Blériot No. XIII.

With no one flying, Blériot had a clear run. He lifted the plane quickly from the ground and crossed the marker line with his engine at full speed. Eight minutes and 42.4 seconds later he had completed the circuit and beaten the previous record easily. As he returned to the hangar, well satisfied with his effort, he saw Glenn Curtiss coming across the field with his golden-colored biplane. He paused,

watched the American take off, and waited for the result
with a grim smile. His record was short-lived—a few minutes only—for the American had lowered it by 7 seconds.
Blériot shrugged his shoulders—there were five more days,
and his next flight would surprise them all. Before the day's
flying finished, sixteen others had qualified for the following Saturday's main event, the Gordon Bennett Trophy.

The light was beginning to fade when Lefebvre took
his Wright biplane into the air again and showed the crowd
how easy it was to fly. He was applauded on each circuit,
flying as near the stands as he dared to give the paying cus-
tomers a good exhibition for their money. He was fast becoming the most spectacular of pilots, and his dives brought
shouts of delight from those present, with many a squeal of
fright from the ladies as he pulled the plane from within a
few feet of the ground and zoomed upward again.

So ended the second day of the Reims meeting. The flying
had improved with the weather, and if it continued fair
and dry the following day's visit by the President of France
would set a high tone to the week's enjoyment. It would
also give an added zest to the designers and builders of the
planes who were now looking for fresh fields to conquer.

It was, as one editor wrote after attending the first day's
flying, "conversion by sight." Throughout the world the international newspapers were reporting what was happening near the historic cathedral city in northern France.
"Flying records were being broken. It was fantastic to see
the flying machines banking and climbing so easily—several at a time without mishap. Earlier that week there were
seven planes flying simultaneously. 'Men,' the newspapers
declared, 'were flying with gasoline engines no more powerful than the motor-car which anyone could see on the streets
in ever increasing numbers.'"

The journalists were in their element describing the scene

at Reims. Photographs gave readers a graphic view of what was happening, to prove to the world that flying was a fact and no longer a dream. Men were flying every day, and many were up in the morning and afternoon, too. People could see for themselves how simple it was. Even the objectors, grudgingly admitting that men were flying in competition, went on to compare them with motorcars, the horseless carriages, as they were called. "Motorcars will soon be filling the roads and racing at thirty miles an hour, and, if not stopped, these flying machines will soon be filling the sky."

The year 1909 had been a memorable one for flying, a year of many firsts. The first aeronautical exhibition had been held in London—the Olympia Aero Show—with eleven full-size planes on display together with aero engines made by Green, Renault, and E.N.V. There was also the new French Gnome, a rotary engine which was destined to become world-famous during World War I. In July, Louis Blériot became the first man to fly across the English Channel from the European continent over that all-important narrow strip of sea. It was a feat that was but a prelude to what was to come. Now, in August 1909, the world was watching the best of the flying machines in direct competition for even larger prizes at the world's first aviation meeting. With the President of France, Armand Fallières, and several of his cabinet ministers promising to be present, the efforts of the organizers gained such prestige and distinction that others were attracted.

Cortlandt Bishop, president of the American Aero Club, who had persuaded Glenn Curtiss to compete, represented American official flying circles. From England came Roger Wallace, chairman of the Aero Club of Great Britain. Lord Northcliffe represented the British press. The official

deputation from Great Britain was headed by David Lloyd
George, the Chancellor of the Exchequer. He was bringing
the chiefs of staff of the British Army to join with the
French Minister of War, General Le Brun, and his army
commanders. But the main center of interest was not the
political or military visitors, but the planes, nearly forty of
them, of various designs.

There were biplanes and monoplanes. The biplanes were
called pusher planes because the propellers were behind the
wings and the pilot, while the monoplanes were called
tractor planes with their propellers in front of the wings.
Blériot was there with five monoplanes, and Voisin had
nine biplanes. The Wrights were represented by seven biplanes, all made in France under license. The Farmans
had four, and, like the Wrights, these were biplanes.

That week, from Sunday morning until flying finished on
the following Sunday, the arguments were profuse. Everyone had his own ideas and preferences: Which was better—the monoplane or the biplane? Was the Blériot monoplane faster than the Antoinette monoplane? Which had
greater stability in flight? Would the Curtiss show it was
the speediest of the biplanes both in takeoff and in the
air? Would the Farman carry more weight, and would it be
easier to land or stay up longer in rough weather? Would
the Wright plane make a name for quickness in making
turns and prove more robust in structure? The controversy
continued to the final day and beyond. Each plane had
features superior to others; no one had them all. But the
meeting did show that despite the bad weather at the beginning of the week and the winds that continued until the
last two days, these flying machines had advanced further
in every way—safety, speed, performance, and reliability—
than even the most optimistic person had realized.

Captain Ferber still retained faith in Gabriel Voisin's skill and long experience in building biplanes and attributed his inability to get his plane off the ground to his own short-comings. He continued to give Voisin all the political help possible.

Cockburn from England started the week with one per-fect circuit in his Farman biplane, and Latham was again in the air. While Latham was flying, four other pilots suc-cessfully flew the 30 kilometers necessary for the speed prizes, and their circuit times were all very close; only 1.5 seconds divided the first three. Since these were all Wright biplanes made in France, it did much credit to the two pioneer American airmen after the original doubts that many had expressed. Not only were fast times recorded, but others were making exciting flights to enthuse the specta-tors.

Strange as it may seem now, the Wright brothers still continued to launch their machines from a small wooden truck running along a sixty-foot-long metal track. They were fearful, they explained, that the skids or runners which acted as landing gear, or undercarriage as it was later called, would, when taking off, dig into the rough ground, especially after rain. This led to many an argument among the expert and knowledgeable men present—"Which was better, skids or wheels?" Despite the arguments, the Wright licenses kept to the skids and launching track while all the other plane builders preferred to see their machines bump along the uneven field before taking off rather than put up with the inconvenience of the metal track and supporting trolley. One thing was noticeable. The Wright plane had the quickest takeoff, even if the skids and track were not so practical.

Lefebvre had no inhibitions. In his French-built Wright he waited with the others as they surveyed the wet and

soggy ground. The absence of wheels never bothered him.
From the beginning of the meeting he set out to demonstrate
the ease and simplicity of flying, and from the moment he
landed at the end of his first flight he became France's most
popular pilot. Unknown before the meeting, his daring
exploits roused the onlookers to heights of enthusiasm. He
was acclaimed by everyone, even his competitors, and was
now accepted as one of the world's best fliers.

Lefebvre had flown for a short time in Holland before
coming to Reims, but now at Reims he had won his "wings."
He pased competing planes, circling the field in a series of
hawklike swoops. He flew under the more experienced
Louis Paulhan with only a few feet to spare. On one such
dive, just skimming the ground, he made many onlookers,
including press photographers, fall flat on their faces as
they feared the worst. No one delighted the crowd more
than Lefebvre. He flew fast double turns, swinging into
tight circles and figures of eight. He was cheered in the air
and surrounded on the field as he walked back to the hangars. Lefebvre took all the glory in his stride. His youth and
daring captivated everybody and made the Wright biplane
more famous than it was before. With only a 25-horsepower
French B.&M. engine, he demonstrated its maneuverability
and easy handling.

Lefebvre, more than any other pilot, converted the doubt-
ers to the certainty that man could really fly. He showed
that man could emulate the birds. The fact that a plane
could fly fast, could fly high, could take a passenger or
passengers, or fly across country meant nothing to the
ordinary man when compared to the antics or stunts, as
they were called, by this carefree man. When the Reims
meeting ended, only Glenn Curtiss approached Lefebvre's
popularity among the thousands who had the excitement of
being present.

Two weeks after Reims, this popular flying star's luck suddenly ended. Taking too many chances in a plane that was not designed for such stresses and strains, his Farman biplane dived into the ground and crashed. Lefebvre was found dead in the wreckage—the first pilot to be killed while flying. His flying life was all too short, but he made more conversions to the ease and practicability of flying than probably anyone else.

Flying was no serious problem, as the pilots at Reims had shown. The next step would be to build better and faster planes for sale. For the airplane builders, winning prizes would be secondary to that of using their experience in making their machines more robust. The world had accepted the motorcar as a means of transportation; now it was up to the inventors to provide another—the airplane. Foremost among these were the Farman brothers, the Voisin brothers, and, of course, Louis Blériot, who would go back to his factory at Pau and produce even better planes than the XII or XIII. But first he had to win one of the speed prizes —especially the American-donated Gordon Bennett Trophy. This would give him the boost he felt necessary.

When he arrived at Reims in the late summer of 1909, Louis Blériot was thirty-seven. He was born at Cambrai, where the first tanks were sent into action in the 1914–18 war. He dominated the European flying scene, and his fame had spread to England and Germany. He was not unknown in the United States. The Wright brothers were good friends of his, and it was through Blériot that they finally set up their factory near Pau, when they left Le Mans. Only Henri Farman and Gabriel Voisin ranked in the same dominant position in France.

Louis Blériot had a friendly, gregarious nature and an affable smile. Like Voisin, he sported a large black moustache, which for many years was almost a trademark. He was calm, modest, seldom upset, and his easy, polite manner won him many friends. He looked upon flying as an outlet for putting into practice the ideas his genius constantly devised. That they were not always successful did not deter him from looking for further innovations to add to his creative work.

Blériot's introduction to flying was, like the Wrights', Farman and Curtiss, through his interest in transportation. The Wrights manufactured bicycles. Farman sold motorcars, Curtiss made motorcycles and small gasoline engines. Blériot joined the automobile world through the accessory side of the industry, inventing a reliable and powerful lamp that quickly became popular. He was wealthy enough to start its manufacture, and this, like the Wrights, gave him the necessary finance to further his interest in flying. Selling other accessories to the motorcar trade brought him in touch with Ernest Archdeacon, Deutsch de la Meurthe, and Gabriel Voisin. He took no active part in the motor racing in which Henri Farman became so popular, but speed and flying had always fascinated him.

Invited by Archdeacon in 1905 to watch the first trials of the Archdeacon-Ferber glider, which Gabriel Voisin had built for them, Blériot decided then and there to get Voisin to build a plane for him. Blériot had studied at the École Centrale des Arts et Métier, and he had several new ideas on airplane design. He did not like the Chanute-Voisin straight wings, even with the slight curvature of the upper surfaces.

After the failure of the first machine which Voisin had built for him and which had crashed in the Seine, Blériot insisted on a new design with annular rounded lifting surfaces for both wings and tail unit. Not for him the cellular box-kite type of plane which had been developed by Chanute and Wright. "It should be made," Blériot said, "of two cylinders with a connecting fuselage. Curves are better than flat planes. What better curves can you have than a cylinder?"

Blériot was disappointed when it failed to fly but still held to his annular idea. He accepted Voisin's box-kite wing but insisted on an annular tail unit for his third plane— the Blériot III. But this, like its forerunner, was also a failure, and reluctantly Blériot accepted Voisin's designs for the more conventional wings. Chanute and Wright had proved them airworthy, Voisin said, so why change?

From May 1906 Blériot concentrated his efforts on designing a succession of planes changing the engine or using two when he thought one engine was not giving him enough power. The Blériot IV was no better than No. III. No. V flew but only in short flights, extended hops that gave him hope for the future. His car accessory company was providing him with more than enough money to make all this work possible.

Blériot was greatly helped by his wife, who encouraged him in his early efforts when others were not so enthusiastic. Madame Blériot, like the younger Madame Paulhan, was pretty and always fashionably dressed. She was vivacious and natural, following Louis wherever he went—even to England. At Reims she was his constant companion and would even have worked alongside him if he had allowed her to do so.

Blériot, as Voisin declared later, was an excellent mathematician. He had the superiority of good breeding, but this did not prevent him from working side by side with his mechanics and meeting them on their own level. Blériot's partnership with Voisin lasted two and a half years—never really compatible, their only bond was aviation and the fact that Blériot could provide finance. Yet as Blériot said later, referring to the first year of his association with Gabriel Voisin when they were working on their early machines, "They were the happiest days of my life. We lived day by day in surroundings that brought only pleasure and satisfaction."

The partnership ended early in January 1908 when Blériot decided to concentrate on building his own monoplane in his own way and without Voisin's help. The widely held differences between the biplane and the monoplane could not be easily overcome.

To Blériot the change to monoplane marked a great advance in flying over his first tractor-type machine. None of his earlier planes, which he numbered I to III, was airborne; only the Blériot IV had ever left the ground and that only in a series of short hops and never satisfactorily.

All these failures, involving months of work and financial loss, merely compelled him to work all the harder, until his Blériot VI gave him the pleasure of flying for the first time in his own plane. During July and August 1907, Blériot was flying 150 meters (about 500 feet) without experiencing any serious problems. By the end of that year he was flying over 1,600 feet with speeds up to 50 miles per hour. He even experimented with 16-cylinder engines.

Encouraged by his wife, Blériot persevered in his chosen occupation. His Blériot VII was the beginning of another change in aircraft design; for the first time the fuselage was completely covered. It had a four-bladed propeller driven by a 50-horsepower Antoinette engine, which gave him speeds of up to 50 miles per hour. At times he covered longer distances of over ½ kilometer—1,600 feet—a good feat that few had surpassed at that time. He built others with mediocre success until he built his Blériot XI. With this he had at last created a monoplane which gave the world—in the summer of 1909—a vision of what was to come. He tried engines up to 100 horsepower but found them either too heavy or too powerful for the slender craft made out of

waterproofed fabric, steel tube, ash, and bamboo. This was
the plane in which he flew the English Channel in July
1909. It had a span of only twenty-five feet and was not
much more in over-all length. Yet with an Anzani 3-cylin-
der 25-horsepower engine he was able to fly at 45 miles an
hour.

Blériot's first real success came in July 1907. His No. VI,
named *Libellule,* or Dragonfly, gave him many satisfactory
short flights, the longest being almost 500 feet in August
1907. A month later he beat this by over 100 feet and
established himself as a successful airplane builder. His
works at Issy-les-Moulineaux were getting too confined,
and he began looking around for a larger place and one
with better flying facilities. But he stayed at Issy until
1909 when he moved to Pau in the French Southwest.

It was while he was at Issy that Blériot constructed his
first plane with tandem-mounted cantilevered wings. It had
vertical surfaces consisting of a long fin and rudder, and
while nothing like this had ever been attempted before, it
proved moderately successful. The No. VII showed a
marked improvement in design and flying characteristics. It
was a significant step forward and gave Blériot speed and
stability which he had not known before. As he exclaimed
to his many friends, "I have at last accomplished what I set
out to do. I can fly faster than anyone. I can balance my machine. I am ready to fly anywhere." This at the end of 1907,
was no small achievement. Blériot's fastest time exceeded
50 miles an hour on most flights; it was something that
brought him much pride.

When he built his No. VIII, Blériot used ailerons for
the first time. He had given up the idea of a large tail
plane as too dangerous when landing, replacing it with
sufficient tail surface to take an elevator and rudder section.
The ailerons were attached near the wing tips, but he

modified these later by fitting them to the wing as flaps, the first flap-type ailerons ever used in a monoplane. Before long Blériot was flying over 700 meters and at last was able to attempt his first cross-country flight, in October 1908, of 17½ miles. Such was Blériot's progress in less than two years after leaving Gabriel Voisin and concentrating on building his own machines.

Established as a builder of monoplanes, Blériot's next move was to exhibit three of his machines in which he embodied new ideas, at the first Paris Air Show of December 1908. The Blériot planes which were shown in the Salon de l'Automobile et de l'Aeronautique were the Blériot IX—an improvement on the VIII bis—and his X and XI. In the IX he had fitted a 100-horsepower Antoinette engine. For an experiment Blériot designed his No. X as a pusher biplane, but this was a failure and never flew. Of the three, only the Blériot XI enhanced his reputation and brought him fame and prestige far above anyone else, whether as a pilot or a builder of planes.

After the December Air Show was over, Blériot, now with orders to fulfill, showed his No. XI's superiority. Flying at Issy, he was using a smaller engine, the R.E.P. 30-horsepower engine driving a four-bladed metal propeller. Early in April he replaced the R.E.P. engine with an even smaller Anzani 25-horsepower unit, and this was proving very satisfactory. Another change was the reversion to wing warping in lieu of aileron control, following the Wright brothers' idea.

In August 1908 Wilbur Wright had startled a skeptical world by flying at Le Mans racetrack, his first flight in France. It was not a long flight—Wilbur stayed in the air for a little more than a minute and a half—but when Blériot saw the elder Wright bank and turn in figures of eight with ease and dexterity, Blériot declared with enthusiasm, "For us in France and everywhere in the world, a new era in mechanical flight has begun."

Blériot, who had become friendly with Wright, was one of the few who had staunchly defended the American. As he told one of his dubiously minded friends, "Wright knows what he is doing. He will fly when he is ready." This friendship was maintained, and when Blériot moved to Pau, near the Pyrénées, it was not long before Wilbur Wright followed and opened his own works near that famous French beach resort of Biarritz.

After Wilbur's triumph at Le Mans in August, Blériot gave up ailerons for good. His action was indicative of those early days of flying, that the successful fliers were always ready to make changes they felt were necessary.

After severing his partnership with Gabriel Voisin, Blériot relied mainly on one man, Louis Reyret, who started as a mechanic and was soon in sole charge of production. Blériot was not a classically trained engineer, but he knew when a plane was giving satisfaction or knew immediately when there were faults. He had many ideas—too many, it was thought. His design drawings were almost unreadable, but he had an instinctive ability to recognize what was good and just as quickly discard the impractical. In those days it was the mechanics, the carpenters, and other assistants who enabled many a pilot to attain success by the innumerable little improvements which men like Blériot could only outline in conversation, or give a descriptive explanation of what they thought necessary. Nevertheless, they worked well as a team, and although the boss got all the praise and the glory—after all, he found the money—the others had the satisfaction of seeing the plane they had constructed fulfill their hopes.

Blériot was a generous man and gave good bonuses when he was successful. In those days the association of

Blériot and his small staff was that of a family and, for
the most part, a happy one. Accidents, and these were
frequent, added to the mechanics' burdens; it did not take
much to damage a machine during those Reims' days. A
heavy or bumpy landing, an engine failure, or even the
overturning of a plane on the ground by a sudden gust of
wind resulted in men having to work all night as well as
by day—and there was no overtime then—to make sure
the plane was ready for the next flight.

Money, except to men like Santos-Dumont, was not
plentiful, and so much was needed to build a plane that
every effort had to be made to conserve expenses and to
find new ways of earning it. So they gave tuition. Many
flying schools were introduced during 1908 and 1909—
and the lessons were not cheap. One crash and the tuition
fees were gone in a moment, especially when an engine
was irreparably damaged.

There were still two schools of thought over the engine.
At Reims, about half the engines were water-cooled and
the others air-cooled. For most of that year the Gnome
rotary, air-cooled, was a welcome newcomer to the scene.
It needed far less space than the stationary engine and
was lighter—a very important factor where power and
weight were concerned. Only a few planes like Robert
Esnault-Pelterie's monoplane (the R.E.P.) used a four-
bladed propeller, while one, the Bréguet, had a three-
bladed one. The conventional propeller was two-bladed.
Bréguet later became known for his fast and reliable monoplanes, a leading fighter and bombing airplane during the
1914–18 war. Engine speeds at Reims varied from as low
as 450 r.p.m. for the Wright biplanes to an average of
1,200 to 1,400 for almost all the others. Blériot preferred
500 r.p.m., although one of his trials was made at the
higher speed. Another cause of controversy was the con-

trast between the warping controls of the Wrights and the aileron controls of such leading builders as Farman, Curtiss, and Blériot. It was clear that aileron control favored by Voisin was steadily gaining in popularity.

At Reims in his preparations for the first day of the meeting Blériot relied on his XI. He had more than one of these, for reserves. He also had his No. XII, the first of a completely new design which he hoped would be more powerful and easier to control, but it was not yet finished.

There was no doubt about Blériot's popularity when he took off at Reims for the first time. He was greeted with cheers that recognized his achievements. The newspapers reported his every appearance, in the city or on the ground at the Bétheny field. His fortuitous successful flight over the English Channel for the *Daily Mail* prize, made when he realized Latham was stranded by the weather at Calais, was still fresh in the mind of everyone at Reims. It was indicative of Blériot's nature—"Now or never" or "he who hesitates is lost." It was such decisions that so often made a pilot successful in those years before World War I, when flying men were determined to succeed.

Reims gave Blériot a new venue. Here he was entering a different environment. Latham would be seeking revenge, and thirty keen fliers, to whom success at Reims meant so much, were getting ready to take the honors and the prize money. There would be no more jumping off while another slept. Latham, who had not flown in the short speed race on the first day, now took the opportunity of taking off early that Monday morning while the weather was good. He was flying Levavasseur's reliable Antoinette IV, which had proved superior to the Antoinette V or VII. Latham's plane had one of the largest wingspans and wing area of any of the monoplanes present. It was powered with Levavasseur's 50-horsepower 8-cylinder water-cooled engine.

Its wingspan of forty-two feet was six feet more than Blériot's but with no greater motive power, it could not compete in speed.

Before the day's flying was over, Latham could not go faster than 9 minutes 13.8 seconds for the one (10-kilometer) lap, which Curtiss had already flown in 8 minutes 35.6 seconds. This was 6.8 seconds less than the time returned by Blériot earlier that afternoon.

Farman had already flown the single-circuit in 9 minutes 6.6 seconds, but Bunau-Varilla, after his earlier troubles in the oat field, clocked a poor time of 13 minutes 30.2 seconds. It showed that speed was not a Voisin characteristic; in fact, the Voisin biplanes had shown little promise of success during the first two days, with the exception of Paulhan (who was soon to change to a Farman biplane). Voisin's nine planes were mediocre in performance, but whether this could be attributed to the pilots or the planes it would be difficult to assess.

At Reims, with so many planes competing, the great problem was finding the best method of starting and getting it off the ground quickly. Concrete runways were unheard-of then. All they had was a fairly flat field that was often used as grazing land for cattle when there was no flying. There were diverse views. It depended on one's prejudices and friendships. The Wright biplanes still used the track and rail but now without the starting weight to propel the plane forward. The Wright biplane could get away quickly and smoothly in the muddy conditions at Reims.

The airplanes at Reims had to be pulled across the field, usually by a string of mechanics assisted by any onlookers, and there were always plenty of such helpers. A local farm horse was sometimes used to plod slowly along, pulling the bulky, cumbersome-looking framework of wood and fabric to the starting point. And motorcars were in keen demand, too, when the ground was dry.

Moving planes from one place to another was always a problem, especially for the big Farmans, Wrights, and Voisins. Once in a while, when the field was particularly dry, they managed to cross the field under their own power. The wind was a great factor in this, as a plane could be quickly overturned or swing to one side unless enough men could hang on to the wing tips or the tail plane. Blériot and Curtiss, with their smaller planes, seemed to be indifferent to the buffeting antics of the gusty winds.

Some of the pilots had difficulty getting off the ground. Monsieur Rougier, for instance, spent the whole of Monday afternoon trying to get going. His Voisin biplane seemed underpowered—more like a mule stubbornly refusing to budge from its starting point. And Rougier was not alone in his troubles. At times many machines were scattered across the ground, swinging and scurrying in all directions like so many oversize chickens fluttering about a farmyard. Occasionally one plane would at last succeed in its attempt to rise, only to fall back onto the ground after ten or fifteen feet of air travel. Some were slow to rise, traveling for some distance before their wheels cleared the ground. Curtiss was exceptional, being quickly in the air. His golden-colored plane was amazing in its takeoff. He only needed a short run—often taking less than forty or fifty yards—to become airborne. Farman found it an advantage to have his men hold on to the plane until the engine was up to full speed, and it was no uncommon sight to see his plane start off on its launching run with one or two men clinging to the wing tips almost streamlined horizontally as it moved swiftly over the ground.

That Monday afternoon's flying gave everyone a good exhibition of aerial progress. It was no longer a dream.

With Paulhan in his Voisin biplane and Lefebvre in his Wright, Sommer added his own biplane to the scene, and they were soon joined by others, some for only a circuit or less. With Delagrange, Comte de Lambert, Bunau-Varilla, and Cockburn joining in the fun, it was exciting from everyone's point of view—even the mechanics', who had made so much of this successful flying possible.

Monday ended with an air of hopefulness about the hangars. There was tomorrow, Monday was only the beginning. All they wanted was good weather and no wind. Everyone was looking forward to the third day of the meeting, for Tuesday was the day that the President of France had promised to attend, and with him there would be many cabinet ministers and others of importance. Reims promised a variety of entertainment that few had anticipated.

The Third Day

Tuesday was a gala day for those attending Reims. With President Fallières due in the afternoon, extra preparations were being made. Flowers and plants were added to give color to the grandstands, and flags decorated the course—national flags for the three nations taking part and many more for those the organizers hoped would take a future interest.

The sky was almost cloudless as the sun rose, but while it cheered would-be visitors, it gave little comfort to the pilots and the owners of the planes because the wind was much too strong. There had been hopes for a concerted effort to contest the speed races, particularly the Prix de la Vitesse of 30 kilometers, but with the wind at 20 to 25 miles an hour the pilots were being forced to content themselves with testing the engines and generally preparing for flights later.

The black flags were still flying at noon, and while no flying was expected before the afternoon there was plenty of activity in and around the grandstands. Many automobiles were arriving, and horse-drawn carriages were crowding the area reserved for them. One side of the course was lined with the hundreds of carriages which could not get into the reserved sections, the occupants standing along the rails, watching the mechanics working on the strange-looking machines which were lined up for the President's inspection later.

The President, not to be put off by the possibility that there would be no flying, had definitely promised to be at Reims. At 2 P.M. the wind was as strong as ever, although men and women were still arriving. According to the official timetable, the President and his party would arrive at 4 P.M. and leave two hours later. Everyone still hoped the wind would abate before the President's departure, especially the members of the French Aero Club who were relying on his interest and enthusiasm to stir the lethargic minds of the military leaders into a more active role.

The mechanics, working on their machines in the open field, were using the enforced period of waiting to carry out tests on the bracing wires and checking the engines for speed and performance. For some, the respite enabled them to change a propeller. There was always plenty to do to keep a plane in good trim. To many of the spectators who had paid good money to be present, it appeared to be time wasted. A few, more venturesome than the rest, went inside the hangars, but most of the spectators stayed in their seats within the protective sides of the stands waiting for something to happen and getting more and more depressed as the time passed.

There was a ripple of excitement when the waiting crowd heard that the President was approaching. Gendarmes appeared, and a squadron of cavalry galloped toward the entrance. It was four o'clock, and everyone was now standing to catch a glimpse of the President's party. Monsieur Fallières was welcomed by the Marquis Polignac and the Reception Committee. The President was friendly and anxious to meet the fliers who had assembled for the official greeting. His gray, bushy beard gave him a distinguished appearance as he smiled with characteristic sincerity. He was well liked in France and was keen to give this new phase of aeronautics official recognition. His official interest was needed in a world of scoffing and an unwillingness to accept change.

The wind was still high when the President was escorted through the various hangars. He encouraged the pilots and laughed happily with such individual makers of the planes as Blériot, Voisin, and Farman. He visited all the sheds and expressed his greatest interest in the monoplanes. The American ambassador introduced Glenn Curtiss, who could speak only a few words of French. The President was likewise unable to converse in English, but their conversation was cordial and good-humored. He spent some time with Curtiss and amiably referred to the Stars and Stripes draped over the high doors of the American's hangar before going inside the shed and carefully inspecting the golden-colored plane.

Curtiss was very pleased with the speed he had attained the previous evening. He had broken the record, but while he knew his time might soon be reduced by another, and he recognized Blériot's machine as capable of fast speeds, he was satisfied with what he had accomplished so far. He told the President he had a good chance of winning the speed race.

All this took some time, but it gave the President a closer view of the planes and a good understanding of the aeronautical progress that had been made since he had assumed his high office three years before. Farman, Voisin, and the Ariel Company's Wright planes were all visited in turn. The French military staff were prominent, following the President and joining in many of the discussions. Their presence gave the airplane builders a wonderful opportunity of pressing their claims for a more active interest by the government.

There were many visiting politicians with the President including Lloyd George from Britain accompanied by a military delegation from the British General Staff. The presidential party by this time had increased in number, and a large party followed the President from shed to shed. All this took some time: there was so much to see and so many people to meet, which of course gratified those concerned, but as the proceedings dragged on, the crowd in the grandstands and around the field grew increasingly restless and bored.

Meanwhile Madame Fallières and the ladies of the party, the wives of the cabinet ministers and others, had taken their seats and, like the crowd around them, were waiting for the President's return. When he finally took his seat, the wind surprisingly dropped, and to everyone's delight the black signal flags were quickly hauled down. An hour had passed since he had arrived, and the impatient spectators were at last happily settling down to see the first of the planes in the air.

More planes were being brought into the field in preparation for the judge's signal to start. Engines were started, some soon at full speed, others coughing intermittently while the mechanics made adjustments. Bunau-Varilla in his Voisin was like a greyhound straining at the leash with men hanging on to it waiting for the "all clear" flag to be hauled to the top of the flagstaff.

He was quickly off the mark, the first to take the air that late Tuesday afternoon. As the signal flags indicated, he was competing now for the single lap of the speed race—

Prix de Tour de Piste—10 kilometers, a little less than 6¼ miles. As he flew in front of the presidential stand, he swept off his flying cap and waved it in a salute with a nonchalance that amused everyone. Others, like Paulhan who followed, thought it was protocol for them to do the same. So flying caps were doffed even after the President had gone.

This same Bunau-Varilla later became the first of the World War I pilots to become a prisoner of war. It happened early in the fighting when he was flying a Voisin bomber during a raid on Ludwigshafen. He had as a passenger General de Goys, the Chief of Operations of the French General Staff Headquarters. They were forced to land in German-held territory, but their plane was undamaged. Captured uninjured, the general managed to escape, but poor Bunau-Varilla was held prisoner throughout the war, from 1914 to 1918.

But at Reims in 1909 Bunau-Varilla was at the beginning of his aeronautical career. He was a natural pilot, handling his big Voisin with its 50-horsepower 8-cylinder E.N.V. engine like a master. Forced down the previous day by the gusty wind into that field of oats, he was soon pulled out and quickly flying again.

As Bunau-Varilla landed, Louis Paulhan took off, "dipping" his plane in salute to the President. He made a complete circuit of the field, never going far from the grandstand, so that the President would have a good view of the flying.

Paulhan was not given to exciting flying, and while he was still banking around the judges' box and the nearby pylon, the presidential party decided it was time to leave. Paulhan's time, competing for the Prix de la Vitesse, was so slow that instead of landing he ignored the judge's decision and continued flying in tight circles above the President.

As the line of cars drove from the course toward the railway station, Paulhan accompanied the party, the first time any President had ever had a flying escort. It gave the President a good view of the Voisin plane to compensate for the limited flying which bad weather had enforced.

Once the President had left, and in spite of a strong wind, the business of competing and qualifying for selected races took a new start. Latham in his Antoinette No. 13—his lucky number, as he told Levavasseur—made an attempt on the 30-kilometer race. But his three laps took 32 minutes 49.8 seconds, far from good enough for that day. Blériot, Latham's cross-Channel rival, took off while Latham was still flying, demonstrating that his monoplane was the faster of the two. Flying in the Tour de Piste, Blériot broke the speed record for the single lap, bringing the time down to 8 minutes 4.4 seconds—about 47 miles an hour.

Dusk was ending the flying, and most of the planes were already in their hangars, but to the delight of those who were intent on staying until the last moment, Lefebvre decided to give another demonstration of aero acrobatics. He darted across the field, banked sharply in double turns, always flying near the stands. His figures of eight requiring steep turns and close cornering were not only dramatic but very exciting to the crowd who had seen so little flying that day. When he finally came down, the cheering was astonishing; the crowd stood clapping, shouting, waving hats and handkerchiefs. Lefebvre's final demonstration was something they had never seen before.

To summarize the day's flying, apart from Lefebvre's dazzling display, what impressed the critics most was the ease with which the pilots handled their machines. No crashes had occurred in spite of the weather and the strong crosswinds. The doubts of the military critics could now be

dismissed. All that airplane builders needed was official
co-operation with orders and, where necessary, financial
aid so that new and better planes could be built. They were
showing at Reims that aeronautical progress was not
merely imagination but a fact. In the first three days, three
makes of aircraft, the Wright and Farman biplanes and the
Blériot monoplane, had given outstanding performances,
while the Voisins and Antoinettes, although overshadowed,
had still made good flights. They could point to Curtiss,
and though he was not French, his demonstrations of speed
and reliability still proved their point, and the next five days
would give further proofs of what could be done.

Reims had two facets, the outward exhibition of flying,
or what the public saw from the grandstands on the large
open space that bordered the racetrack, and what was happening in the hangars, where all the work was done to ensure the planes were airworthy and ready for the events.
Flying did not consist only of mere effortless gliding
through the air or being carried aloft by the power of an
engine. Actual flight was, in these early days, the result of
almost continuous inspection: adjustment, repairing and
checking engine parts, looking for loose nuts, tightening
wire stays, tapping struts, and testing the strength of the
doped fabric that covered the wings and tail planes. All this
was essential before a plane went up and, in most hangars,
immediately after it came down.

By the summer of 1909 the pilots, with few exceptions,
had learned that the foreman of mechanics was in charge
when the machine was on the ground. The pilot might help
where necessary, but the foreman gave the orders. It was
always a delight to any mechanically minded aviator to
watch the systematic way in which the foreman and his
limited crew worked. Nothing was missed—they climbed
everywhere like agile monkeys. Often the engine was dis-

mantled, the propeller removed, to ensure that all would be well and in working trim when it was next wheeled out of the hangar. One had to admire their loyalty and integrity.

Until the spring of 1909, flying was very much experimental. Men like Louis Blériot had given little thought to flying for prize money. Some local communities had been seeking publicity by offering these fliers of heavier-than-air machines small but satisfactory payments. A demonstrative flight over their towns was called a *grand prix,* and men like Blériot and Farman were becoming interested in these air flights. By June 1909, Reims was in the offing. Blériot had been given preliminary notice of the event and had talked with Archdeacon and Ferber. They told him that the "flying week" would be sure to attract all the best pilots and airplane builders. The prizes, they added, would be generous and worthwhile to those taking part, so Louis Blériot began looking around for the extra money he needed to prepare for competition.

In October 1908 the owner of the London *Daily Mail,* Lord Northcliffe, always a keen supporter of flying and a good publicity seeker, had offered a prize of £2,500 to the first pilot to fly across the English Channel from coast to coast. He was hoping to encourage such early British fliers as Horatio Phillips, who had been flying in southern England since the spring of the previous year. A. V. Roe was also a contender, using first a Wright type of biplane and then in 1908 a biplane of his own design.

Robert Blackburn completed the trio of English fliers. He had worked with the Wrights before returning to England to build his own plane. In this he was successful. He built and flew with moderate success his own monoplane in the North of England; it was similar to the Antoinette monoplane—the similarity being mainly in the tail plane—

but it differed with its underslung landing gear in which
the pilot sat, much like Santos-Dumont's Demoiselle. However short though it may be, none of these men was ready
to risk a flight over the sea at that time.

The northern part of France and the southern counties
of England were always subject to unpredictable weather.
It could be fine, there could be storms, the wind could
change over night from a breeze to a gale. This July of
1909 was no exception. Between fog and drizzle, gusty
winds prevailed over the coastline and that narrow strip of
sea. The Northcliffe prize was still unclaimed—it was a year
since it had been offered. Then not one, but two contestants
gave notice of competing for the prize; Hubert Latham,
backed by Léon Levavasseur and his Antoinette Company,
and Comte Charles de Lambert, a wealthy flying enthusiast with two Wright biplanes, which he had recently pur-
chased after the Wrights had taught him to fly.

At last, on July 19, the drizzle ceased, the foggy conditions vanished soon after dawn, and the weather was ideal
for flying. As the sun rose, Latham took his Antoinette into
the air and headed for the French coast, not far from a
French destroyer waiting to escort him across the Channel.
The stage was set. A wide swing and he was on his way,
flying over the cliffs near Sandgatte with nothing but sea
ahead and the beach below.

It was a perfect takeoff, and his thrill of triumph gave
him great delight. He looked down at the sea, now calm
and clear, but his joy was short-lived. The engine began to
misfire, and before he realized what was happening, the
monoplane was gliding down toward the water. Not far
ahead, those aboard the French destroyer heard the sudden
change and saw Latham's rapid descent. As he hit the water, they were already turning and heading for the unfortunate pliot.

As Latham explained later: "My motor stopped. I tried desperately to find the cause without any success. Whatever it was, the carburetor or ignition, there was nothing I could do but glide down. The water was smooth and I slid slowly into it as the engine gave a final cough as if for one last effort. The destroyer reached me within minutes with the monoplane safely afloat like a cork bobbing up and down in the slight swell. I did not even get my feet wet; the wings and tail plane were keeping me afloat until I was pulled to safety."

With the plane salvaged, but in no state to be used for some weeks, Levavasseur telegraphed his factory for another plane to be sent to Calais at once. There was still time to fly the English Channel and even at this late stage to win the prize.

When Blériot heard that Latham had failed, he lost no more time but flew at once to Calais and established himself at the nearby village of Les Baraques, using a farm as his headquarters. While Blériot was at Calais, Comte de Lambert arrived with two Wright biplanes.

Blériot's journey to the French coast was not without trouble. In winning 2,000 francs for a cross-country flight from Étampes to Orléans, Blériot's Anzani engine flashed back. Luckily the plane had not caught fire, but Blériot's left leg had been burned, and he was forced to use crutches as soon as he alighted. He was still using them when, on the morning of July 25, he decided to fly across the Channel.

A gale was still blowing across the little village of Les Baraques the night of the twenty-fourth when the two French pilots, Blériot and Latham, and their mechanics went early to bed with little hope of flying the next day. While they slept, the wind dropped, and shortly before dawn, Blériot was awakened with the good news that a flight was possible. Hurriedly dressing, Blériot, always ready to seize an opportunity, was soon with his mechanics watching them pulling his plane onto the field near the French beaches.

Still using his crutches, unable to actively assist in the preparations, he urged the workmen on. His wife was with him. She had joined him a few days before and hoped to travel by boat to England to be with him when he landed. As the sun rose, the monoplane was in position and ready to take off. So, while Latham still slept, Blériot tossed his crutches aside and climbed into the plane.

"I shan't need these," he told his wife as he kissed her. "If I cannot walk, I can fly. I'll meet you in Dover."

As Madame Blériot and her party hurried toward the harbor to board the boat and with Latham sleeping, Louis Blériot took off from the Les Baraques field and headed for the Calais coast a few miles away—and toward the white cliffs of Dover twenty-three miles distant on the other side of the English Channel.

Half an hour later Blériot was shaking the hand of a solitary English policeman as he climbed from his pilot's seat, standing happily on English soil below the castle on the cliffs above. The reporters were soon gathered round— they had been warned of his coming and now were listening to his graphic story.

"At 4:35 I gave my mechanics the order to 'let go.' The machine rose splendidly. My course to the sea lay across the sand dunes, and then I had to surmount the telegraph wires which run along the coast.

"After circling the plain I struck across the dunes, and went over the telegraph wires at a height of about a hundred eighty feet. I could see the destroyer *Escopette* a few miles out at sea as soon as my monoplane was in the air, and as she was to steam toward Dover I took my bearings from her.

"The destroyer was steaming at full speed, but I very quickly passed her. My machine was then traveling at about forty-five miles an hour, the revolutions of the propellers being about twelve hundred to fourteen hundred a minute. Whilst traveling over the Channel my monoplane was at a height of about two hundred and fifty feet. At times she dipped a little, but I then pumped in some more gasoline and worked the apparatus which causes the machine to rise, when the monoplane soared up to two hundred and fifty feet again. I wished to keep the monoplane at two hundred and fifty feet, as that would be suitable for the landing at the point on the cliffs which had been selected. The machine would have no difficulty in soaring to much more than double that height.

"For about ten minutes after I passed the destroyer I was able, by looking back, to steer my course by the direction in which she was steaming. Then I lost sight of her and everything—the English land was not in view.

"I decided that the best thing to do was to set my steering gear for the point at which I had last seen the *Escopette* heading. This done, the flight continued for about ten minutes, with nothing in sight but sea and sky. It was the most anxious part of the flight, as I had no certainty that my direction was correct; but I kept my motor working at full speed, and hoped that by following the direction I had got from the destroyer I should reach Dover all right. I had no fear of the machine, which was traveling beautifully.

"At last I sighted the outline of the land; but I was then going in the direction of Deal, and could see the long beach there very plainly. In setting my steering I had overlooked for the moment the effect of the wind, which was blowing rather strongly from the southwest, and had therefore deflected me eastward. I could have landed at Deal, but I had started to come to Dover, and made up my mind to get there. I therefore headed my monoplane westward, and followed the line of the coast to Dover about a mile or a little more out at sea. I could see a fleet of battleships in Dover Harbour, and I flew over these to a point where I could see my friend Monsieur Fontaine, with a large French tricolour, denoting the point where I was to descend. I flew over the cliffs all right, but the descent was one of the most difficult I have ever made. When I got into the valley between the castle and the opposite hill, I found an eddying wind. I circled round twice to ease the descent, but alighted more heavily than I had expected to, and the monoplane was damaged."

Madame Blériot concludes her husband's description of his flight: "It was a very trying time as we steamed on and on, with neither coast in sight, and what an agonizing moment it was when presently the officer reported that the *Escopette* was steaming back toward us.

"Happily, however, it was only to report that my husband had succeeded. Oh! then I felt the happiest woman in the world! When we got to Dover, there was my husband waiting on the quay to meet me and tell me himself of his achievement. It was splendid."

The damage to the monoplane was not serious. Little mattered now that Blériot had accomplished what he had set out to achieve. Joined by his wife later that morning, he quickly became the center of the world's praise—"the world's greatest flier." The Wrights, Farmans, Voisins, and the rest were obscured behind the façade of journalistic acclaim. The French were particularly delighted with the result of this brief, thrilling, and pregnant flight. The British were no longer the islanders they thought they were. This time it had been the English Channel. When would it be the Atlantic?

As one newspaper commented reviewing the day's happenings: "What M. Blériot can do in 1909, a hundred, nay a thousand will do in five years time. . . . A machine which can fly from Calais to Dover is not a toy but an instrument of warfare which soldiers and statesmen must take into account." This prophetic statement was made just five years before World War I.

(There is an interesting aside to the occasion. Never before had a customs official been called upon to deal with the arrival of an aircraft. But the Dover customs officer was equal to the occasion. Although rules existed only for ships, the regulations still had to be adhered to. The customs officer treated Blériot's plane as a yacht, and M. Blériot as the owner and master. There was also the problem of quarantine, and the following certificate was thereupon issued: "I hereby certify that I have examined Louis Blériot, Master of a vessel 'Monoplane,' lately arrived from Calais, France, and it appears by the verbal answers of the said Master to the questions put to him that there has not been on board during the voyage any infectious disease demanding detention of the vessel and that she is free to proceed.")

When news of Blériot's departure reached the Latham-Levavasseur camp, Latham hurried to his new Antoinette in a final attempt to catch Blériot. But by the time they had wheeled the monoplane into position, the wind was blowing into a gale. Latham had been beaten again, this time by the wind. He stood there silently gazing across the Channel, his head bent, his eyes blurred. For two weeks he had maintained a fighting spirit, but after his forced landing in the sea and now with Blériot on his way to England, he was left bereft of hope. He sat down slowly, dejected and bitter, almost in a state of collapse.

Now at Reims, only four weeks later, with spirits regained, encouraged by the indomitable humor and self-confidence of Levavasseur, Hubert Latham was prepared to take on Blériot once again in another contest.

These previous encounters intensified the struggle for supremacy. With records being broken daily, the pilots at Reims were as keen as ever to show France and the world what they could do.

The Fourth Day

Wednesday began as the worst day of the week. At dawn it was raining, almost a deluge. There would be no President of France to attract the crowds today, and black clouds were threatening the pleasure of even the most ardent flying enthusiast. Fewer people had arrived at the Bétheny racecourse than on the previous days. The surrounding fields were empty. There was a cold wind, unseasonable for August. The heavy rain kept the pilots and mechanics well within the confines of the sheds.

The rain stopped during the morning, and a watery sun managed to give a little brightness to an otherwise miserable scene, but toward noon black clouds darkened the sky and rain again fell at intervals. As usual it was not the rain that prevented flying but the wind, which at times blew hard in gusts of 20 to 30 miles an hour. The Grand Prix was on the program and its postponement was not unexpected as the wind continued.

Curtiss watched the sky hopefully. He had lost the speed record to Blériot the previous day after seeing his fast time of 8 minutes 35.6 seconds reduced by Blériot to 8 minutes 4.4 seconds. "Give me half an hour this evening," he remarked, "and I will bring the record down below eight minutes." His hopes improved as the afternoon hours passed; soon after four o'clock not only had the rain stopped, but the wind had lessened considerably until only a light breeze was blowing and flying became possible after all.

The black signal flags came down, and at last the red flag was hoisted to the masthead giving the cheerful sign to the few optimistic arrivals. One machine was wheeled into the open, Paulhan's Voisin. Several others followed Paulhan's example, but although the air conditions were good, none of them was able to leave the ground. Paulhan, however, wasted no time. As he waited while the machine was swung into position, he declared optimistically, "I am not coming down until I have covered at least a hundred and fifty kilometers." His 50-horsepower air-cooled Gnome was quickly started and in full power in a matter of minutes. Without delay, Paulhan's Voisin rose gracefully into the air to make his attempt on the Grand Prix. His was the first flight of the day.

For some time Paulhan was alone in the air, often out of sight of the onlookers. The monotony was broken at last when Latham in his Antoinette and Fournier in a Voisin also rose above the field. Yet Paulhan still continued to attract the crowd's attention whenever he passed the grandstands. The signals given in the program informed them that he was flying for the Grand Prix and would even try for the world's long-distance record. Each circuit brought it nearer.

While he was flying, the sky became dark with large black clouds scurrying overhead; it seemed as though a terrific storm was about to break, but Paulhan flew on. Luckily the sky cleared slightly, and with a break in the clouds, patches of sunlight crossed the racecourse bringing a succession of rainbows to tint the scene.

As Paulhan approached the long-distance record made by Wilbur Wright in the previous December, the excitement grew intense.

At last, as he finally passed Wright's record, the crowd cheered and clapped to show their pleasure. This well-deserved greeting was acknowledged by Paulhan waving his hands in a return salute. Twenty-three minutes later, having flown 131 kilometers, 82 miles, Paulhan was well ahead of any other competitor for the Grand Prix and the holder of a new world record. His flight surpassed anything seen in the first four days, and when he glided down to earth, there was a rush toward his machine. Soon it was surrounded by his mechanics and as many spectators as could get past the watching gendarmes.

Not content with this great feat of endurance, Paulhan waited for Voisin to cross the field by automobile, carrying more gasoline, and with this, the pertinacious flier again took to the air and flew back to the Voisin shed. As he jumped down from his seat, Paulhan received another long and enthusiastic cheer from the nearby stands and reserved enclosures. Cold and tired by his prolonged effort, Paulhan nevertheless acknowledged the vociferous welcome which greeted him as he walked slowly back into the hangar behind his machine. For him the day had not been wasted.

While Paulhan was up, Latham made some attempts on the speed record, but they were not good enough. He took off again, hoping to exceed Paulhan's record, but gave up after flying for only 31 kilometers. After Latham's landing, Fournier and Captain Ferber, "M. de Rue," took off. Ferber's takeoff was a lucky one, as his machine had not given him many flights that week.

Fournier was not so lucky. He traveled only a few kilometers when, after making a good turn at the far end of the course, he made a sudden dip toward the ground. Already that week he had crumpled one of his plane's wings, caught by a crosswind, and now the same thing happened again. Flying too near the ground, the plane swerved, one wing tip caught the ground and turned the tail high into the air. Seconds later the nose of the plane crashed into the ground.

Fournier was lucky to escape injury—he emerged only slightly cut and bruised—but his plane was severely damaged. The tail collapsed, broken by the fall, and one wing was completely smashed into a twisted mass of splintered wood and torn fabric. Fournier's mishap ended with characteristic friendliness. A mounted gendarme arriving on the scene a few seconds later, seeing Fournier walking around the crashed machine, with a cut across his nose but obviously not injured, jumped to the ground and persuaded the somewhat dazed pilot to take his place in the saddle. Minutes later, while mechanics hurriedly took care of the somersaulted plane, Fournier, shaken but indomitable, rode back to the hangar with surprising aplomb, to the cheers of those standing nearby, as though he were a conquering hero.

Yet Fournier was annoyed. "If all those *veillottes*," he said, referring to the haycocks that had been left in many parts of the field, "had been removed, this would not have happened. We were told all the hay would be taken away before the flying meeting started. Look at all the fields around the course, with wheat, barley, and oats cut and standing in bunches to dry. My accident might have been more serious. Someone might yet be killed."

This was true. Fournier's crash demonstrated the danger

of flying with an untrustworthy motor over a country covered with obstacles.

Another plane was in the air to keep the crowds happy in between the intermittent appearances of Paulhan—who, with his long circuits, would fly steadily past until the evening skies began to darken. It was Hubert Latham in his Antoinette monoplane. This was a good day for Latham. If Wednesday could be called anything, it could be named Paulhan and Latham's day. Few fliers had been out, and only those two were successful in their attempts. Latham had a special reward as he made his third attempt to break the record for the Prix de la Vitesse. The rain had passed and a watery sun was shining across the field when, as Latham turned toward the grandstand, a magnificent rainbow appeared across the black clouds beyond and arched over the slender Antoinette—holding it in a spectacular frame unique for its rareness.

While Latham failed to beat the Prix de la Vitesse record, Glenn Curtiss, encouraged by the Antionette's flight, decided to make his only effort for the day. He had to beat Blériot's excellent time made the previous day for the fastest lap, but as the days passed, he became more and more conservative with his machine and himself. He had spent a lot of money to get to Reims. He had hotel bills to pay and mechanics' wages which went on even if there was no flying: maintenance was necessary, and there were minor repairs to consider every time the biplane did go up. There was gasoline and oil to pay for and no one but Glenn Curtiss to foot the bill. So he went up only when the conditions were safe, if not ideal, and never when dangerous. This late afternoon gave him every hope, and he decided to make at least one attempt to beat Blériot's time, the record set the previous day. No one else was attempting the Tour de Piste.

His optimistic hopes were not fulfilled. After a few cautious runs up and down the course, with the light fading, Curtiss decided to try for one lap and only one, equal to 10 kilometers, almost 6¼ miles. No one had yet broken the 8 minutes' time; Blériot's best was 8 minutes 4.4 seconds. Curtiss wasted no time. At full speed he roared down the course, banked swiftly, then pointed his plane back again toward the judges' box. Eight minutes and 11 seconds later he came down with a landing that surprised everyone, even himself, making several short hops before coming to a stop. By then it was dark and he had failed again. With a grim smile he strode into his hangar without looking back, leaving his men to follow with the gold-painted machine.

If Reims did one thing, it seemed to imbue a spirit of friendly competitiveness among those taking part. There were no quarrels among the pilots or the aircraft builders. If anyone was ready to take off, he would have plenty of help to enable him to do so. There was order, not interference, and this helpful attitude enabled the officials to keep the meeting going smoothly. Even the press and photographers could feel this co-operative understanding and responded accordingly.

Just before the Wednesday's flying ended with Curtiss's late attempt on the speed record, Delagrange took his Voisin biplane up for a short flight without accomplishing anything startling. He was a safe and steady flier, never gaining any popular standing—in fact, he was not too well known outside flying circles. Delagrange was Voisin's first customer after Blériot severed his association with Gabriel. He once became piqued with Voisin's apparent closer co-operation with Henri Farman, but he soon overlooked this action. He paid Voisin handsomely for work done—often overpaid—and never grumbled. He was an artist and sculptor, and knew nothing of dynamics, but had been a flying enthusiast for some years and was always quite willing to pay for any plane that Voisin built for him. Delagrange was not being very successful at Reims, but that could only be attributed to his ultra-carefulness, taking no chances and trying to break no records. He loved to fly, but not too fast or too high, and was not yet ready to risk a cross-country flight.

After Delagrange's flight, Rougier and Captain Ferber took up their Voisin planes but did nothing spectacular. Of the Voisin camp only Louis Paulhan showed any success, but he, unlike the others who came directly under Gabriel's influence, was of a different caliber. Captain Ferber, who had not been very successful during the first days of the meeting, flew several times on that Wednesday, but he too was, as always, quite content to give the spectators a demonstration of safe flying and leave it at that. Ferber flew as De Rue, which served his desire for anonymity. Between them the Voisin pilots demonstrated the reliability and structural ruggedness of the Voisin biplane, and this gave Voisin as much satisfaction as winning prizes.

There were others of this flying era, pioneer pilots of dominant reputation, who had similar feelings about winning prizes and had failed to attend Reims. They were the Wright brothers and Alberto Santos-Dumont.

"I have other things to do," said Wilbur Wright when asked if he would go to Reims for the Flying Week. "I am not interested in prizes. I am only interested in building and selling airplanes. Let others amuse themselves by racing if they want to."

Santos-Dumont was equally disinterested, but for other reasons. He was by nature more of a recluse and preferred to be left alone, shunning publicity. "I am too busy experimenting with my latest Demoiselle," he explained to the press. "I cannot go to Reims."

Although he did not attend the Reims Flying Meeting, Santos-Dumont was indirectly greatly concerned with its success. His numerous accomplishments were an integral part of French aviation history. His photograph was shown on the front pages of the newspapers whenever the subject of aviation became predominant. There were always stories about his balloons or airships and, since October 1906, his exploits in his heavier-than-air powered airplane. He first amazed France and the world when he made the first airplane flight in France, the first to fly after the Wright brothers. But he preferred to keep away from the public eye and never encouraged interviews with the persistent pressmen.

Alberto Santos-Dumont had been a wealthy young man. His father died when he was eighteen, and although born in Brazil where he had spent his early youth, Alberto had finally decided that Paris was where he wanted to live and devote his life to aeronautics. After his first balloon ride, flying became an obsession. Santos-Dumont became a unique individual with no close friends.

Apart from a short attendance at Bristol University in England for a technical and scientific course, he spent his whole life in Paris. By 1897, when he was twenty-three, he decided he had learned enough. He suppressed occasional yearnings for Brazil, and, back in Paris, ballooning once more became the lure to entice him above the crowded streets of the cities and into the peaceful solitude of space.

Alberto never allowed himself to look other than a wealthy well-dressed man of the town. Individual in taste and appearance, almost jaunty in style, he maintained a characteristic smartness whether he was in his hangars at Neuilly or in Maxims in Paris. He was distinguished by his fastidious headgear and was seldom without a hat outdoors. When flying he wore either a straw hat or a derby. He sometimes permitted himself to relax in a Panama thin straw hat that flopped about his somewhat elongated features, yet even the floppy hat gave him a superior air. Frock-coated always, his topcoat almost touched the ground. On one of his early balloon trips he arrived on the scene wearing a light-colored topcoat that almost covered the white spats over his ankles; a large flower in the lapel of his jacket completed his dapper style.

From youth he sported a moustache always neatly trimmed, and unless roused by a disturbing incident he made no effort to show his feelings. Taciturn, never given to much smiling, he nevertheless could mix socially, when he was in the mood. But he preferred small groups to a large party. He was fully conscious of his small height, being only 5'5", but never let himself be overawed by anyone taller. To him, when his aptitude for flying excelled, his lack of height was an advantage: he could stand in the cockpit of an airplane as he had always done in his airship or balloon. As an acquaintance remarked, "Alberto goes about in a dream. He sees little of the world about him, and nothing of those nearby."

Yet his face was a strong one; he had determination, even obstinacy, when in a crisis. His hair was brown, as were his eyes; he brushed his hair slickly with a middle parting that individualized him as different from others. In spite of his neat, almost de rigueur attire, Santos-Dumont was never a fop; his clothes were only an outward covering for a keen, analytical mind that could quickly get to the core of a problem or, by continued scientific mechanical elimination, create the product he felt would give a satisfactory answer.

After his first balloon ride his enthusiasm for ballooning never waned, even when he had changed to the airship. "I often long," he said, "for the peace and utter stillness of the drifting gasbag with no motor to jar one's susceptibilities."

But Santos-Dumont had to progress; he had the inventor's constant drive to something better. Another Frenchman, Henri Giffard, in 1852, had made an elongated balloon and, having invented the steam injector, fitted a 3-horsepower steam engine to drive his "airship," as he called it. Others copied Giffard; the Tissandier brothers in 1883, Charles Renard and Arthur Krebs in 1884. Now, in Germany, David Schwarz was building a rigid airship with a framework of light aluminum alloy—the forerunner of the Zeppelin. Santos-Dumont, learning of this, immediately decided to build an elongated balloon that could steer and be independent of the wind.

"To me," he said, "simplicity is everything. . . . Complications repel me."

This first airship was fitted with a 3½-horsepower gasoline engine which he adapted to his nonrigid airship with the help of a motorcar mechanic, Albert Chapin. The airship was 25 meters (82 feet) long, and flew for the first time in September 1898 using hydrogen, 180 cubic meters at a cost of one franc a cubic meter.

It is amazing what he was able to do with such a flexible bag of hydrogen gas. When he first tried its airworthiness, it was steered without difficulty, in spite of its length, responding to every movement of the rudder; fortunately, there was almost no wind.

No. 1 was followed by another slightly larger, which he also flew in 1898. In 1901 he made a great name for himself with his No. 6, in which, after several failures, Santos-Dumont won the Deutsch Aeronautics Prize of 150,000 francs by flying from St.-Cloud, outside Paris, around the Eiffel Tower and back to St.-Cloud in half

Cover of Reims program *(Science Museum)*

Gordon Bennett Trophy *(Musée de l'Air)*

Blériot monoplane in front of grandstand *(Royal Aero Club)*

French spectators in front of Reims grandstand *(Musée de l'Air)*

The course at Reims *(Musée de l'Air)*

President Armand Fallières of France (with beard) in reviewing stand *(Musée de l'Air)*

Buffet in grandstand *(Musée de l'Air)*

Planes lined up to take off *(Musée de l'Air)*

Paul Tissandier's Wright biplane on takeoff tract *(Musée de l'Air)*

Orville Wright making the first flight at Kitty Hawk, North Carolina, December 1903 *(Science Museum)*

Lawrence Hargrave testing his first box kites, Australia, 1895
(Science Museum)

One of the last flights of Otto Lilienthal *(Science Museum)*

Gabriel Voisin's powered glider on the Seine, 1905 *(Science Museum)*

Gabriel Voisin at controls of his biplane *(Smithsonian Institution)*

Ernest Archdeacon, "father of French flying" *(Musée de l'Air)*

Captain Ferdinand Ferber ("De Rue") preparing to board his Voisin biplane *(Royal Aero Club)*

Étienne Bunau-Varilla and his Voisin biplane at Reims *(Royal Aero Club)*

Blériot IV, 1906, with annular tail-lifting surface, at Lac d'Engien
(Musée de l'Air)

Hubert Latham being rescued from the English Channel, 1909
(Musée de l'Air)

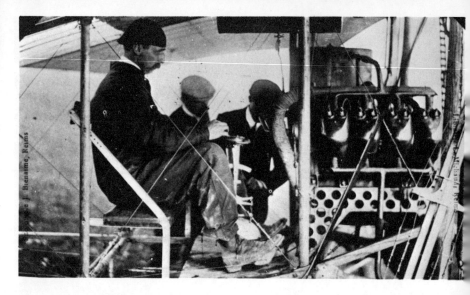

Louis Blériot at the controls of his monoplane at Reims *(Royal Aero Club)*

Louis Blériot's monoplane at Les Baraques-Calais before crossing the English Channel, July 15, 1909 *(Musée de l'Air)*

Louis Blériot arriving at Dover after crossing the English Channel
(Musée de l'Air)

Alberto Santos-Dumont making the first powered flight in France, 1906 *(Musée de l'Air)*

Alfred Leblanc and his monoplane *(Royal Aero Club)*

an hour. This brought him international fame and much
prestige.

During the early years of this century, Santos-Dumont's
airship works at Neuilly was the scene of constant activity,
by night as well as by day. Many well-known Parisians
constantly visited the huge hangar, and it became the
center of a growing society of interested sportsmen, politicians, and visiting international figures. Archdeacon, Ferber, and Deutsch rarely missed a weekly visit to watch
the progress of his latest airship. Blériot, a friend of Ferber's and Archdeacon's, took a lively interest in the proceedings, and before long Henri Farman, brought by his
brother Maurice—an ardent balloonist friend of Ferber's
—also joined the distinguished company.

During 1904 and 1905, Santos-Dumont started to build
first his No. 13 and then No. 14. The first was to have
its own heating plant to generate hot air to fill the bag—
it never flew—but by then Santos-Dumont was beginning to have second thoughts on the heavier-than-air machine, and when he was completing No. 14, it was already
assuming a strange appearance. By then, Alberto Santos-
Dumont had met Gabriel Voisin.

From early 1905 until late in 1906, Gabriel Voisin had
been concentrating on improving the glider which had
crashed on the Seine and developing the possibilities of
putting power into it. His experience on the Seine, using
a motorboat to pull him off the water into the air, was
fraught with dangers, solely because the heavier-than-air
machine became entirely dependent on outside power.
Voisin gave up any idea of using this method, deciding that
the power unit must be within the glider. It was at this
time that Voisin had contracted to build a biplane for
Delagrange, the artist-sculptor, to be fitted with a 50-
horsepower Antoinette 8-cylinder engine. While this was

being built Voisin had another visitor, Alberto Santos-Dumont.

The secrecy with which Santos-Dumont surrounded himself was never lessened in his dealings with Gabriel Voisin. No one knew what Santos-Dumont had in mind, but it was understood he was building the framework for a powered unit to be slung under the belly of his latest airship, No. 14. This was a semirigid airship with a good lifting capacity. It was different from any he had previously built, having a load-carrying girder slung much farther below the envelope. It brought much criticism from those who knew Santos-Dumont. Said one, "Your weight is too low and in the wrong place. You will never be able to control it and it is too long. You will pull the airship down."

But Santos-Dumont revealed nothing when he replied, "I know what I am doing and you do not. That's the difference between you and me. This is a different airship and built for a purpose. My Number Fourteen will always be remembered."

Santos-Dumont was right but not in the way he anticipated. What was remembered was not the airship—No. 14 —but the appendage he had slung underneath the gas-filled envelope. The appendage was quickly known as the "14 bis"—the word "bis" meaning additional. His idea was to attach a power-driven heavier-than-air machine to the airship to give greater directional control and more positive power to the lighter-than-air dirigible above.

Voisin's influence on Santos-Dumont was unquestionable. He it was who had followed through with Octave Chanute's description of the Wrights' glider. With only meager knowledge, since the Wrights were secretive to an intense degree, Voisin managed to design his first glider, and from that the others followed. Voisin was a conscien-

tious inventor, using Chanute's glider of the Indiana sandhills; there is no doubt that Gabriel Voisin indirectly copied
the Wright biplane, since the two sprang from the same
common source—the Hargrave box kite. Voisin was
another French flier who had no knowledge of the Wrights'
powered plane and, in fact, would not believe the Wright
brothers had flown a powered airplane in 1903.

There are many, in France and of course his native
Brazil, who are today convinced that Alberto Santos-Dumont was the first to fly a powered heavier-than-air plane
and that the Wrights' so-called flights at Kitty Hawk were
only hops, due to the uneven surface of the sand dunes.
Gabriel Voisin did nothing to disprove it. He, in fact, encouraged the statement without equivocation, but somehow
Santos-Dumont kept aloof from the argument—as would
be expected from one whose whole attitude to life and the
general public was one of superior intelligence, above any
such mundane arguments. What he had accomplished was
there for all to see. The arguments were epitomized by one
statement which to a Frenchman gave its own answer:
"Why did not the Wright brothers enter for the Archdeacon
prize in 1906 for a simple straight flight and why did
they not refute Santos-Dumont's claim to be the first to fly?"

No one challenged this argument, foolish as it was, even
when photographs were shown and proof was available
for anyone who wanted it. The real facts are that no one
in France wanted to see proofs at that time.

At last the "14 bis" saw the light of day as a separate
unit. Nothing like it had ever been seen before. It had the
appearance of two box kites, and soon became known as
the Canard, because the elevators were in front. The box-
kite wings were rigged, or placed, at almost ten degrees
of dihedral and not, as in previous gliders, at right angles
to the fuselage. But the center of gravity was somehow in

the right place, and, to give Santos-Dumont the credit due for careful design, he knew what he was doing. The 14 bis when first seen gave a false impression of its stability. Its only control was the elevator, and if it was a freak, as many alleged it to be, this freak, the brainchild of Voisin and Santos-Dumont, did fly, and what is more it was the first airplane to fly in Europe under its own power.

When first seen with its powered unit securely attached to airship No. 14 by a cage of all-embracing ropes, the strange combination was at once ridiculed. "A monstrous hybrid," someone called it, gazing at the gasbag pointed at both ends and the strange-looking addition slung underneath.

When the day came for airship 14 to make its first flight, the engine was started and the airship, with its 14 bis attachment, was released from its moorings—although the ground crew were still holding some of the ropes. Instantly all was confusion, with Santos-Dumont shouting "Let go" while the swarming overanxious mechanics were still hanging on to the ropes. Some ran forward, some to the side, with Santos-Dumont trying desperately to gain control.

But the dual contrivance refused to fly freely. It bobbed up and down, it swayed, it pitched and tossed, the engine roaring to add tumult to the shouts of the crowd and the screams of those tangled in the snakelike ropes. It lurched on the guide rope, and the much flaunted demonstration of Santos-Dumont's skill would now have to be shown if catastrophe was not to end the day's effort. Somehow, in the center of the rolling, careening envelope, Santos-Dumont managed to bring order to the confused men below him on the field, and peace once more reigned.

There was nothing more to be done that day, but Santos-Dumont had already made his decision. Back inside the airship hangar, 14 bis was separated from the airship and prepared for its own individual flight without the attachment of the incongruous gasbag. On September 13, 1906, a few weeks later, the 14 bis, to give it its official name, with Santos-Dumont again at the controls, was rolled out for its maiden flight. In close attendance were Gabriel Voisin, Ferber, and Archdeacon, with a crowd of onlookers most of whom waited with misgivings.

That it flew at all was a miracle, yet it did so, and the lightweight 24-horsepower Antoinette engine had just enough power to lift it off the ground as the officials of the Aero Club threw themselves on the wet grass to make sure the wheels did rise into the air. No one was really satisfied that day, especially Archdeacon. The plane was wheeled away without winning the prize of 3,000 francs he had offered in 1904, for the first heavier-than-air powered aircraft to fly over 25 meters.

Never defeated, however, Santos-Dumont brought out his 14 bis again a few weeks later, on October 23, 1906, and this time with double the engine power, another Antoinette, he achieved success. There was no doubt this time. He won the Archdeacon prize by a good margin, actually flying 60 meters, almost 200 feet, in 7 seconds, with the wheels well above the ground in a perfect flight. Everyone cheered as Santos-Dumont stood there unperturbed, handling the controls with gloved hands, knotted tie, and impeccably cut suit. He could have been the captain of an oceangoing liner as he became the first man in France to fly a powered plane.

He was completely oblivious of the excited crowd of officials, photographers, and reporters as the flight ended. He watched them as they swarmed toward him, more than a little frightened as they rushed into the path of his descending machine. The motor cut out when he was a foot above the field, and the next moment the plane touched the ground, swaying precariously, bumping and jerking to a hard landing. But before the plane had come to a complete stop, the strain was too much for the undercarriage support. Its wheels collapsed slowly, very slowly, as it tilted over to one side with one wing resting on the earth, the other slanting into the air.

Santos-Dumont climbed down from his elevated position of aeronautical power into the arms of the onlookers as they grabbed him and excitedly carried him on their shoulders toward the happy, beaming Ernest Archdeacon.

"Have I won?" he asked. "Tell me, have I won?"

What could the much revered Archdeacon say? What could anyone say? Santos-Dumont, first so many times, in balloons and airships, had done it again. He repeated the flight on November 12, to show his earlier two flights were not flukes. The 14 bis in spite of its strange appearance could fly. He flew for 21 seconds over a distance of 220 meters, 722 feet, at a height of over 20 feet, and for the first time he used his aileron-balancing control—an octagonal unit in each of the outer wing cells. It was simple: the control wires from each aileron were fastened to a body harness, so that if one wing dipped, Santos-Dumont had only to lean in the opposite direction to bring the machine back to an even balance again.

Santos-Dumont copied his ailerons from Esnault-Pelterie's 1904 glider, which, in turn, was probably based on Matthew Piers Watt Boulton's British patent of 1868, forty years earlier. When Santos-Dumont fitted the ailerons, although crude, to each outer cell of his box-kite wing, he found his balancing control was greatly improved. He was the first to use an aileron-control lever—later called a control stick and, still later, a joy stick. The operation was simple. By moving it laterally the pilot could raise or lower the aileron section of the wing. If the stick was moved forward or backward, it controlled the elevator to send the plane into a descent or a climb.

Two years later, Blériot copied Santos-Dumont, and Henri Farman followed, placing the ailerons to suit their ideas of balance. Eventually Curtiss, plagued by the Wrights for patent infringements, made a similar change when he realized the advantages of maintaining this quick, almost instantaneous, balancing control. Yet few people today, apart from a handful of the older or "early fliers," know of the debt the world owes to Santos-Dumont for the use of the aileron, on which every airplane depends.

It was a pity, everyone agreed, that Alberto Santos-Dumont did not attend the Reims Flying Week of August 1909. Whether it was through pique or just indifference, no one will know. He did as much as, if not more than, anyone to make it a success; he led the way in France, if not in Europe. His innovations have been declared fundamental to modern flying, and yet he decided not to be present. Perhaps he felt he would not reign supreme above his fellow pioneers. Adulation was such a part of his success that to give way to another, or even stand on the same pedestal, would be anathema to him. It was more than he could stand. He preferred to stay away and to glory in his undoubted successes of the past.

His Demoiselle was his next effort. The huge cumbersome biplane with its long fuselage in front was too reminiscent of the Voisin box-kite theory and quickly became obsolete in the mind of Santos-Dumont. It is uncertain whether Santos-Dumont knew of Blériot's work on lighter aircraft, but the two were certainly working along the same lines at the same time. Blériot's first monoplane had cambered wings covered with varnished paper. It was wrecked soon after its first flight. Santos-Dumont, never hurried, continued in his own way, and although his Demoiselle may

not have flown until two months or so after Blériot's Nos.
VI and VII, it was without doubt the world's first successful light aircraft. It weighed less than 240 pounds. It
was made of bamboo and had a fan-type tail. The pilot
sat underneath the center of the wings and controlled the
rudder and elevator situated in the tail, which was the
forerunner in design of Levavasseur's Antoinette.

After his success with the Voisin-built biplane Santos-
Dumont realized that the biplane was all right as part of
an airship to provide motive power with stability, but as
a separate unit, to fly on its own, it did not fit into his
ideas. What was needed was a smaller single-wing machine more like the hawks that soared overhead, which
gave grace and beauty and yet strength in flight. He would
design his bird-plane himself and not be influenced by
Voisin or any other. With that in view Santos-Dumont once
again withdrew from the outside world to concentrate on
the new idea—the monoplane—the first successful design
of its kind.

Santos-Dumont, genius and benefactor, would not let
his main desire, to benefit science, be overshadowed by
anything else. He was generous to a fault. His inventions
—the lightweight engine which he had had made by Alexandre Darracq, the design of the Demoiselles, the aileron
features—were for all to use. He did not forget his contemporary pilots in their hour of triumph. After Louis
Blériot flew the English Channel in July 1909, Santos-
Dumont wrote to him with a genuine feeling of good
wishes: ". . . It is a victory for the air over the sea. . . .
Thanks to you, aviation will cross the Atlantic."

Santos-Dumont did not have to go to Reims. His spirit
was there. The planes, the pilots, the designers, the organizers, were able to demonstrate man's mastery over the
air because of his indefatigable obsession to fly and become

the only man who ever held a pilot's license for all four types—balloon, airship, biplane, and monoplane. He wrote his own obituary: "I have flown every type of machine."

He flew a Demoiselle for the last time three months after Reims. He then passed into obscurity. Twenty-three years later, a sick man, still a recluse, he ended his life in tragic circumstances. If only he could have flown at Reims, what a triumph it would have been, but he wanted it otherwise.

The Fifth Day

At last the weather at Reims changed, and dawn on Thursday, August 26, was clear and bright. From sunrise until noon the air was calm; at no time was the wind more than a gentle breeze, and at times not a leaf stirred. With the better weather, everyone expected a day of thrills and good flying. Spectators began to arrive soon after daybreak, and as the morning sun brought a feeling of satisfaction to the crowds, most of the planes came onto the field, their owners delighted. The red signal pennants were flapping at the top of the flag masts. The parking area was alive with automobiles, their owners taking advantage of the good weather. The grandstands were filling, and again the fields around the racecourse were black with hundreds of men and women ready for a day's outing—lunches packed and everyone in a happy frame of mind.

The Bétheny meeting still had four more days of excitement before the last plane would glide to earth. In spite of the bad weather on the first four days, the flying had not been unsuccessful. Races had been held, records broken, and very few accidents had marred the meeting. The planes had showed sturdiness in all but the worst winds. Frail they might look, but as long as the motor functioned, the pilots had nothing to fear. The canvas and wood structures could live in stronger winds than had previously been imagined.

One of the first competitors off the ground was Hubert Latham in his Antoinette. Latham was making an attempt to beat Paulhan's record for the Grand Prix de la Champagne. He spent the morning methodically flying circuits in his No. 13 until the gasoline tank was empty. In a little over an hour he flew 70 kilometers, about 40 miles, but was far from satisfied and decided to try for a longer flight after lunch.

Delagrange was second in the air that morning, demonstrating his Blériot monoplane, which he now preferred to the Voisin biplane. There was nothing spectacular in his flight, but it pleased the crowd. Not too well known by the public, he nevertheless had a reputation for safe flying. He flew low and near the stands so that he would be seen by everybody.

The Englishman Cockburn, who, for all his weight, was a good pilot, was able to show his Farman biplane to advantage. At one time, to add excitement to an otherwise dull period, he raced a passing train, beating the latter and then triumphantly circling it.

For his afternoon flight, Latham, hoping to double his morning's distance, took his Antoinette No. 29, which had a larger gasoline tank than his No. 13. He started well, and 1 hour 3 minutes later he had passed the 70 kilometers mark and was still in good trim. He had flown 100 kilometers in less than an hour and a half, and when his gasoline tank finally ran dry, he had gone 154 kilometers, almost 100 miles, in 2 hours 13 minutes 9.6 seconds, putting him in the lead. When the result was announced, he was cheered enthusiastically by the crowd. The Fates were smiling on him at last and making up for the series of disappointments that had troubled him only a few weeks before when attempting to fly the English Channel.

Blériot, his conqueror then, was not planning to beat any long-distance records at Reims. He was concentrating on the speed races, which were more exciting to his mercurial nature. Once while Latham was flying, Blériot took up a passenger. This gave the crowds a new thrill, particularly as he stayed near the stands flying low in order to lessen his passenger's fears.

Others that afternoon were Comte de Lambert in a French-made Wright and Rougier flying a Voisin, both making short flights. Tissandier, also in a Wright, soon had trouble and was forced to land. Captain Ferber lent his Voisin to Georges Legagneux, while Sommer and Cockburn took up Farman biplanes without incident. Even Curtiss went up late in the afternoon to make an attempt on the Grand Prix, but he made no serious effort to beat Latham's 150 kilometers. After flying 30 kilometers he decided he had gone far enough; he had had his day's outing and he was waiting for the more exacting event, the Gordon Bennett Trophy on Saturday.

The day's flying was a "mixed bag," with nothing spectacular apart from Latham's performance, yet two mishaps marred the afternoon's events. Rougier was flying and completed a circuit when his engine started to misfire. At that time he was not far above the crowd near the automobile enclosure—the *enceinte,* as it was called—and dropping quickly. With quick presence of mind he managed to lift his machine over their heads and without stalling put the nose down again in, luckily, the only open space. With onlookers streaking in all directions he somehow missed the more concentrated places and finally stopped clear of anyone. While it caused the spectators to suffer from the shock of a plane descending in their midst, it gave Rougier a sense of satisfaction to find himself capable of controlling the plane he had designed and built himself and avoiding serious trouble. The weakest part of an airplane, in those days, was its engine, the rotary engines being particularly prone to give trouble owing to the centrifugal forces acting on the valves during rotation. The size of gasoline tanks was also a limiting factor.

Blériot, like Rougier, was also in for trouble, this time with his steering gear. Taking up a passenger for the third time, he failed to make a good turn and for a moment was in a serious predicament. However, with superb skill he managed to avoid a squadron of dragoons which was occupying the middle of the racecourse. To avoid running into the mounted soldiers, he was forced to veer quickly to the side of the course. Seconds later, unable to stop, he had crashed into the fence that bordered the reserved enclosure behind which the spectators were standing. As they saw the machine rushing toward them, men and women scattered in all directions. No one was injured, and although the wheels of Blériot's machine were bent and the undercarriage broken, neither Blériot nor his passenger was injured. The machine was carried into the hangar, but the pilot walked away smiling with relief.

Reims was not Blériot's lucky meeting. The first part of the week had been mediocre, but Tuesday had been a more satisfactory day. He had flown the single circuit of the Prix de Tour de Piste in the astonishing time of 8 minutes 4 seconds, a world speed record of over 45 miles an hour.

Comte Charles de Lambert, one of the lesser known pilots at Reims, had learned to fly at the Wright Aviation School under the terms of the agreement which the French syndicate had made with the Wrights. He gave a good showing at Reims, finishing fourth in the Grand Prix. With him, first at Le Mans in the fall of 1908 and later at Pau, were Paul Tissandier and Captain Paul Nicholas Girardville. They had passed their solo flights in March 1909, but Girardville gave up flying soon afterward.

Tissandier, another of Wright's pupils, added luster to his aviation prowess by starting the first day of the meeting with a flight of three laps, a distance of 30 kilometers, in 29 minutes, to establish a record for the day. Later in the afternoon he also clocked an excellent 9 minutes 26 seconds in the Prix de Tour de Piste of one lap. He more than paid his expenses for those two flights.

Comte de Lambert, who had failed to fly the English Channel in competition with Blériot and Latham, now brought out his Wright wheel-less biplane as evening approached. Skimming along the metal track, he was quickly rising into the air aided by the simplicity of the Wright launching device. This time his engine did not fail, and soon he was circling the field with satisfactory regularity. His main target was the Grand Prix, the distance events, and for some time it seemed likely he would beat Paulhan and Latham. Unfortunately, like so many others who were attempting the long and wearying trial, his gasoline tank was not large enough for the project. After covering 116 kilometers and staying in the air for 1 hour 51 minutes, the gasoline tank was empty, and down he came.

After De Lambert landed, it was appropriate for Louis Paulhan to make certain that his Voisin biplane could carry an additional gasoline tank which he had fitted. The Voisin camp calculated that with this second tank he would have ninety liters of gasoline, about twenty-four gallons, which for his 50-horsepower Gnome rotary engine would be sufficient for a four-hour flight at least.

Engine trouble was always the greatest bugbear. The arguments for and against the stationary or the rotary engine never ceased. There was vibration in the former, and valve trouble through centrifugal force in the latter. The only one who seemed to pass unscathed in this persistent and annoying conflict with mechanical problems was Glenn Curtiss. An engine builder since he powered his first bicycle, his only engine gave him no worries at all during that week at Reims. Curtiss's was the exception. Cockburn, the English pilot, spent more time working on the engine of his Farman biplane than he spent in the air.

Power had always been a great problem, and in 1909 it was still far from being solved. In 1860, almost fifty years before Reims, Étienne Lenoir had invented the gas engine but with no thought of using it for flying—not even for balloons or airships. It was a crude affair and weighty. Sixty years earlier, in 1799, Sir George Cayley, the English scientist, had suggested using a steam engine in a glider but quickly realized it would be too cumbersome and heavy for the purpose. He anticipated the internal combustion engine when he devised his own hot-air or "caloric" engine, as he called it. Yet Sir Hiram Maxim, in 1894, did succeed in fitting a steam engine in a full-sized airplane. He tried two steam engines with an aerodynamic lift greater than the weight of the aircraft and a crew of three, but the experiment ended in disaster.

Maxim's engine had 2 cylinders with cast-steel walls, one tenth of an inch thick. The steam pressure was 320 pounds, which at a speed of 375 r.p.m. developed 180 horsepower. The weight of the airplane was another 6,500 pounds. Sir Hiram Maxim was the first to use a railway track, the plane resting on a trolley. The Wright brothers used this same idea nine years later but with a more satisfactory result. Maxim's plane did actually raise itself from the track, but as it was only a few inches and for only a second or two, a flight could not be claimed. It crashed ignominiously and never flew again. The plane had no pilot so could not be compared with the Wright brothers' flight seven years later.

Of course, the early airships had power enough to distinguish them from the spherical balloon. The Giffard airship of 1852 had a steam boiler and single-cylinder steam engine to drive an eleven-foot-diameter propeller, this being the first attempt to give power for human flight. The airship could travel at a speed of 5 miles an hour. The boiler and steam engine were suspended about twenty feet below the gasbag for safety reasons, and even the stoking door of the boiler was protected by a wire mesh screen. It weighed about 350 pounds.

An earlier lightweight engine for air power was the Stringfellow-Henson engine, of 1842. Although given a $500 prize for the lightest steam engine by the Royal Aeronautical Society of Great Britain, it never reached the actual flying stage. In 1883 the two brothers Albert and Gaston Tissandier built a ninety-two-foot-long dirigible. They used an electric power plant of twenty-four bichromatic-potash cells driving a Siemens motor of 1½ horsepower, but it weighed 600 pounds—a very poor ratio of power to weight, 1 to 400. Its flying performance was not of resounding success, although it did manage to make many flights during those later years of the nineteenth century.

A more successful powered airship was the French-built *La France* in 1884. This had a 9-horsepower Gramme electric motor using chromium-chloride batteries, and Captain Krebs, who piloted the airship, which was 165 feet long and 27 feet in diameter at its center, managed to get a speed of 13 miles an hour. But electric power was not the answer. In 1888 Karl Woelfer was the first to fit a gasoline engine, made by Gottlieb Daimler, into an airship.

Following Nikolaus Otto's four-stroke-cycle engine of 1876 and Karl Benz's high-speed gasoline engine in 1885, the next satisfactory engine was that designed for the Langley "Aerodrome," as Dr. Samuel P. Langley called his flying machine. He took the name from the Greek word *dromos,* meaning a racecourse. The engine built in 1902 was the product of two men: Charles Manly, the designer, and Stephen M. Balzer, the engine builder. It was an outstanding achievement for a lightweight yet powerful unit. Its power to weight ratio was a unique 1 to 4. The stationary radial cylinders, five in number, were water-cooled, and the entire engine, including carburetor, ignition unit, etc., weighed only 208 pounds. It developed 52 horsepower.

The Manly-Balzer engine was the forerunner of the first engine actually used in powered flight under human control, the Wright engine used in 1903. After the Wright brothers had made several successful glider flights in North Carolina, Wilbur decided to build a gasoline engine, light enough for the glider, yet with sufficient power to get them into the air and keep them there. They tried to locate a small engine that would give them about 10 horsepower, but although they contacted all the better known engine manufacturers in the United States, they could find nothing suitable. Automobile and stationary engines were far too heavy. In 1902, when they decided to attempt powered flight, there were only a few such makers of gasoline engines—the Ford motorcar did not appear until a year later. So they decided to make their own.

They had a bicycle factory, and motor bicycles were already becoming popular. What better development would fit into their own works? Their chief mechanic was enthusiastic.

"I cut the crankshaft," he said later, "from a solid block of steel, which weighed over one hundred pounds. When I had finished, the crankshaft weighed nineteen pounds. There wasn't much to that first gasoline engine, no carburetor, no spark plugs, only four cylinders, pistons, and connecting rods. We used the old make and break system of ignition and it worked."

The engine took about three months to build and was first tried in February 1903. There were troubles.

"The bearings froze," said Wilbur, "and the body cracked. Lighter castings were made, new bearings installed, and these did much to solve our problems."

In May 1903 they tested it again, and this time the new engine worked satisfactorily, but they had other problems. Their glider had to be redesigned and rebuilt to take the power unit. More tests. They had made their own wind tunnel some time before, but now corners had to be rounded, struts and braces needed "streamlining" (although this term was not used until many years later). Then another important problem that followed engine power had to be solved. They had to make another piece of equipment to enable them to fly—the propeller.

Orville viewed the development of their propeller as just as important as the engine. It was part of the power unit, yet, apart from the crude examples used by Santos-Dumont in his dirigible, the airscrew, as it was called, was crude and almost useless for their heavier-than-air craft. Four-bladed airscrews had been used by earlier airmen who sought to copy windmills in order to solve their problem.

"We were pleased," Orville explained, "with the results of the tests. We had expected only eight or nine horsepower, but the engine gave almost twelve horsepower and it worked smoothly, without vibration. The dry weight of the engine is over one hundred and fifty pounds, and we still have not produced a satisfactory screw propeller."

So back they went to their wind tunnel. From the earlier airscrews, they did not neglect a ship's propeller in their quest. Many designs were tried, discarded, or rebuilt. Flight lift was the all-important factor, and they carved from solid spars, laminated boards of spruce glued together, using the old adz and knives to shape and smooth the long pieces of wood. Finally they were satisfied, and when they went to Kitty Hawk in the early fall that year, they took with them the first completed power unit.

Other problems quickly appeared, and the question of weight distribution became an all-important factor. If the engine was placed in the middle, the pilot would have to control the plane from the side. Wilbur decided it would be better to lie on the bottom wing and so distribute his weight over a larger area, since the weight of the engine and gasoline tank would be more than the weight of either himself or his brother. To restore the effect of this imbalance, they decided to extend the wing by a few inches on the heavier side, and instead of using one propeller in the center, to use two—one on each side—spinning in opposite directions to correct the possibility of too much pull on either side. To drive the two airscrews from the common engine shaft, a chain and sprocket unit was adapted from the simple wheel drive of their own product, the bicycle. The final weight of their aircraft was 605 pounds.

So much for the Wrights' development of a power unit which enabled them to fly in 1903, but progress after that was slow, and it was not until 1907 that any new development occurred to improve the power unit. In the previous year, Léon Levavasseur, a builder of motorboat engines, had turned to aero engines. He had taken part in the unsuccessful trials of the Archdeacon-Voisin glider on the Seine when one of his motorboats, through inexperience on the part of the man at the helm, sent Gabriel Voisin crashing into the water. Levavasseur saw clearly that towing a glider was no answer to the problem of flight. His experience in engine building enabled him to build an 8-cylinder engine with two banks of 4 arranged at a 90-degree V formation. It was a lighter type of his own motorboat engine.

Levavasseur used direct gasoline injection into the valve ports, the valves being spring-loaded. It was water-cooled, and in the earlier models the water turned to steam but was condensed in a separate tubular condenser. This Antoinette engine developed 50 horsepower at 1,100 r.p.m. and weighed 210 pounds. For Santos-Dumont's 14 bis aircraft, Levavasseur built two engines, a 24-horsepower unit as well as the 50-horsepower. These engines weighed about 3½ pounds per horsepower, an extremely good ratio which was not greatly improved on for many years in this type of engine.

Following Levavasseur's entry into the power side of flying, others soon became interested. Weight was the dominating factor, and air-cooling offered an opportunity to remedy this shortcoming. Two men, Alessandro Anzani, a successful motorcycle manufacturer, and Robert Esnault-Pelterie, who had been experimenting, first with gliders and more recently his own design of a heavier-than-air machine, both produced an air-cooled engine. While Esnault-Pelterie's engine was originally built for his own machine, Anzani's engine was offered to anyone. Blériot was the first to use an Anzani engine, and the 3-cylinder fan-shaped unit proved its reliability on that Calais-Dover cross-Channel flight two years later. The 3-cylinder engine developed 25 horsepower at 1,600 r.p.m., not a great deal but sufficient for Blériot's very lightweight monoplane. Anzani's next engine was later redesigned to give 40 horsepower. Still later he increased the number of cylinders to give a full radial air-cooled engine, with the cylinders spaced evenly around the crankshaft.

The great change in aero engines came in 1907 when Laurent Seguin built the first rotary engine in which the crankshaft remained stationary and 5 radially arranged cylinders and crankcase revolved around it. This was a great innovation, although Lawrence Hargrave, the Australian who had invented the box kite, had worked on a rotary engine before the end of the nineteenth century.

Seguin's engine, which he called the Gnome, was later redesigned as a 7-cylinder radial unit to give 50 horsepower. It was followed by still higher horsepowers of 70, 80, and 100. It revolutionized the flying scene. Many plane manufacturers adopted the rotary engine, preferring it to the heavier stationary engines of equal power. In some ways the rotary engines were difficult to control. The use of castor oil as a lubricant resulted in the pilot being sprayed lavishly with the smelly oil, but the pilot had other and more worrying problems to contend with. The worst of these problems, as far as the engine was concerned, was the failure, due to centrifugal force, of the rotating valves. The largest Gnome engine, used by Blériot and others, had 14 cylinders to give 100 horsepower.

Other rotary engines manufactured during these early years were "Le Rhône" (80 horsepower, 9 cylinders), the Ross-Peugeot (7 cylinders), and a 6-cylinder "Flitz" engine of 60 horsepower, which weighed 91 kilograms (200 pounds). The troubles due to centrifugal force acting on the periphery-placed valves were later eliminated by the single-valve, or "Monosoupape," engine, but at Reims this great improvement had not been invented.

At Reims, Voisin used as many as six different types of engines, the two air-cooled rotary units of Gnome and Renault. The Wrights had their 4-cylinder B.&M. water-cooled 25-horsepower engine, Farman kept to the Gnome and Vivinus—also a 4-cylinder unit but developing 50 horsepower—and Blériot kept to the Anzani and the English E.N.V. engine with 8 cylinders, water-cooled, of 50 horsepower.

The tremendous improvements in engine design were not apparent during those developing years of 1903 to 1908, but when the Reims meeting ended in August, there was no doubt that engines, despite their shortcomings and the inevitable teething troubles, often due to lack of experience on the part of the mechanics, had given aerial locomotion the great boost it needed. Never again could the man in the street scoff at the pilots and manufacturers who had achieved so much with so little outside help. As someone summed up the achievements at Reims: "This was 'ocular demonstration' that no one can refute."

The Sixth Day

If there was one thing that attracted the visitors on Friday, it was the Grand Prix or, as it was billed in the newspapers, Le Grand Prix de la Champagne de la Reims, the greatest race of all time. It was not a race as we think of races these days, but more a feat of endurance—to see who could stay in the air for the longest period during the official hours of flying. Friday was to be the last day for the competitors to be able to attempt to wing the prize. The organizers were hopefully expecting a large crowd.

Many of the pilots and mechanics, with such aircraft builders as Henri Farman, Gabriel Voisin, and Louis Blériot, had spent much of the night in preparing their machines for the contest. New propellers had been fitted, engines replaced, and some had even rebuilt their wing structures to give better results.

The sun rose in a cloudless sky, with only a light wind. The leaves in the trees showed only a slight movement and the signal flags fell limp against the masts. After breakfast, a few light clouds moved slowly across the sky to temper the sultry heat. It was an ideal day for competitors and spectators alike, with most of the crowd staying until 7:30 P.M. when flying would officially end for the day.

At the beginning of the day, the distances recorded during the week for the Grand Prix were as follows: Latham in his Antoinette monoplane, 154 kilometers; Paulhan in a Voisin biplane, 131 kilometers (he had a Gnome engine); De Lambert in his Wright plane and motor, 116 kilometers; Tissandier, also in a Wright, 110 kilometers.

Several would be trying to better their previous distances, while Curtiss and Blériot had decided not to make any other attempt and would reserve their machines for the Gordon Bennett Trophy, the following day. Cockburn from England was still working on his damaged Wright and would also wait for the Gordon Bennett contest. Latham and Paulhan, the leaders, were out early, the latter with enough gasoline to beat any record. Sommer, who held the pre-Reims long-distance, cross-country record with a flight to Bouy of nearly 2½ hours, had only been able to complete 60 kilometers at Reims. He was determined to do better. Plagued with engine trouble since his arrival, Sommer had been working in the hangar most of the night. He had changed the propeller, which he felt was not truly balanced, and with the early morning conditions perfect, he was in the air before the official timekeepers had arrived. He stayed up for an hour and came down well satisfied.

The morning saw every seat in the grandstand taken; the standing enclosures had several rows of onlookers at the rails, and motorcar owners had difficulty in finding spaces in the parking enclosures. As the morning passed, the planes were constantly taking off and landing, to the great satisfaction of the crowd.

Just before noon, with Latham's record still unbeaten,

Delagrange was circling the marker pylon near the sheds, not far from that part of the course where the machines could speed along the ground before takeoff. Paulhan, out to break Latham's record, took off just as Delagrange rounded the corner and lost height. With Paulhan rising and Delagrange dropping, it seemed that a crash in the air was certain. Delagrange was unable to swerve out of the way; he tried to lift his Blériot, but the motor was not powerful enough to take him clear. Paulhan tried to drop back to the ground, but his sudden avoiding action brought one wing down too low. It struck the ground, swung the tail into the air, and, after a partial somersault, Paulhan found the nose of the plane smashed and the machine completely wrecked. Paulhan was thrown clear but badly shaken; one hand was cut, but otherwise he was not seriously hurt. As he stood surveying the scene, he realized his Grand Prix efforts were finished—a disappointment which all shared with him.

Luncheon was taken with the satisfaction that Paulhan had been able to walk away from the crash. Poor Delagrange, disturbed by what had happened, also decided to give up flying for the day and quickly landed to offer Paulhan solace and regrets for the accidental mishap. The arrival of the French Minister of Public Works, Alexandre Millerand, just before lunch, interrupted the program. His keenness to tour the hangars and talk with the airplane owners and pilots caused the crowds to become impatient. They had traveled long distances and paid good francs to see the flying and were not a little perturbed by the official visit.

There was no doubt that the meeting was proving its ability to attract international society from all over the world. Europe, particularly France, was becoming airplane conscious, with flying as the main topic of conversation.

These last three days promised to be a period of special interest, the culmination of spectacular events, which would be remembered for a decade or more. Aviation history was being made at Reims.

To give the spectators an extra thrill and to remind them that the age of the dirigible had not ended, the two dirigibles *Colonel Renard* and *Zodiac* appeared. It was, as someone pointed out, an "aero show," and they were as much a part of the week's demonstration as the heavier-than-air competitors. A special event had been declared for them called the Prix des Aeronauts, and the winner would be the pilot who flew 50 kilometers, about 30 miles, in the shortest time. Their size kept them in view of the racecourse for most of the time, and even though there was nothing exciting about the race, it maintained an interest as Kapferer, a balloonist of the old school, completed the course in 1 hour 20 minutes, 5 minutes less than Henri de la Vaulx in the *Zodiac*. Latham added a little excitement by repeatedly flying under the *Colonel Renard* like a saucy sparrow skimming under an eagle.

The afternoon passed slowly. Sommer, his Vivinus engine now running smoothly, finally got into the air and began his final attempt. Latham went up again as the evening approached, but not long after six o'clock, his supply of gasoline exhausted, he was forced to come down without beating his previous distance. Sommer came down soon afterward, having made six circuits—a little over 60 kilometers—far less than Latham or Paulhan. Farman, who had been circling the racecourse for some time, was now alone. Others had been up and down while he was constantly reminding them that the Grand Prix had still to be won. It was noticed that while the monoplanes flew as high as 40 to 50 meters, even reaching 70 meters—200 feet— the biplanes kept much lower, rarely flying above 50 feet.

Henri Farman postponed his flying until long after lunch when the crowd, after some thrilling flying in the morning, had settled down in the warm sultry atmosphere to watch with somnolent feelings the events of the afternoon. Most of the machines which were still airworthy were taken up, none for any long flights, but more for the enjoyment of flying under ideal conditions. When Curtiss and Blériot had shown what they could do and Tissandier had landed soon afterward, Farman declared his intention to fly for the Grand Prix. He and his mechanics had been working since dawn to complete the installation of a new and more powerful engine, a Gnome rotary 50-horsepower. His Voisin box-type tail unit had been converted to an open plane with twin rudders.

These changes and additions greatly improved Farman's plane, giving it greater power and ease of handling. As Farman took off in his one and only attempt for the Grand Prix, he passed over Sommer, also in a Farman biplane. As he did so, Latham in his Antoinette monoplane added to the thrill by overhauling the other two, all three planes passing each other vertically. Farman took off at four-thirty, but even at this late hour he still had a chance to beat Latham's previous day's record. Knowing Farman's determination, Latham made a final attempt and this while De Lambert was still flying.

If any day could be named for the achievements of any particular flier at Reims, Friday, August 27, could be called Henri Farman's day. His display of sensible, rational flying placed him firmly above the other contestants. Speed and spectacular flying gave way to solidarity of purpose. He passed the first 100 kilometers in 1 hour 41 minutes 47.2 seconds, still flying at an average height of 50 feet, giving a perfect exhibition of steady flight.

It was only a year or so before when Farman, commenting on his earliest attempt to fly, expressed his feelings on the difficulties involved. "To leave the ground," he said, "is not an easy matter, but to fly is still more difficult. I succeeded in leaving the ground every day during the last two months, but it is only recently that I have managed to fly a distance of two hundred and eighty-five meters [350 yards] to beat Santos-Dumont."

Soon after Farman had risen into the air, Latham came down without exceeding his previous mark. Sommer followed Latham and came in to land without beating any records. Farman was now the only one left in the Grand Prix, and he was showing no intention of giving up. Having left his attempt rather late in the day and with only forty minutes to spare before he had to take off, he completed the changeover of his new engine and with only one quick trial was hesitant no longer. It was now or never, and for him, as always, it was now.

Henri Farman had been drawn into aviation through his expert knowledge of motors. The internal combustion engine was still an unknown piece of machinery except to a few. It was a lucky owner if his car did not break down on even the shortest run and have to be towed into the nearest town by a horse or horse-drawn vehicle. This was a common sight in the closing years of the nineteenth century.

Farman was the son of a comparatively wealthy English journalist, the Paris correspondent of the London *Daily Telegraph*. He, like the Wrights and many others, had started selling bicycles and then cars. He soon became known on the French motorcar racing tracks. He loved sport but was not impressed with the future possibilities of balloons or airships. Through his brother Maurice he met Archdeacon, Ferber, and the rest of the small coterie of fliers, Blériot, Voisin, Santos-Dumont, and Delagrange.

A Frenchman despite his name and parentage, Farman could speak only a few words of English. Yet for many years he insisted on signing his name as Henry and even retained British citizenship through his father until he was nearly sixty. In flying he more often used the French "Henri" when naming the biplanes he was later to design and build.

Farman became associated with Voisin when Voisin's finances were at the lowest point. He still had to complete the plane which Delagrange had ordered, and Blériot's departure had not made things easier for them. Farman was financially able, like Santos-Dumont, to indulge in what was soon to be his sole interest in life. He, like so many who had become interested in flying, had graduated (if that term could be used) from motor racing. His arrival at the Voisin works was like a gift from the gods, and Gabriel Voisin welcomed him with open arms. He had money, and he was reasonable in his attitude toward the mechanical side of flying; after all, as he explained, he had been motor racing for almost ten years and this gave him a knowledge of engines that few others in France possessed. It was the one subject that even Gabriel Voisin could not dictate to him about. Soon, too, he was to prove he was a born flier, with a sure instinct for handling the controls of a heavier-than-air machine, even in the most inclement weather.

Farman did not find Gabriel Voisin an easy man to deal with. For some time Voisin had been left to do as he liked when it came to designing and building his biplanes. Archdeacon was only concerned with the end product—his glider and its performance. Voisin had no money troubles with Archdeacon, and having a Frenchman's frugal mind, he made every franc count without a centime being wasted. When the time came for him to leave Archdeacon and he had to deal with Blériot, money was not so free. Blériot, having had as much, if not more, flying experience as Voisin, would not be told by Voisin what to do. There was friction between them over designs, especially over motive power. Finally they parted.

When Blériot left Voisin, the Voisin Frères Company had only a few francs in the bank and they still had to complete the Delagrange biplane for which they had taken an order and were under contract to deliver. Voisin had received a quarter of the cost of the plane, which meant the balance would not be paid until the machine was delivered. Thus, at the beginning of 1907, the Voisins were not in a happy state financially, the biggest problem, as yet unsolved, being the purchase of the engine, a 50-horsepower Antoinette, with 8 cylinders. At this point Henri Farman appeared.

Farman had a fine personality and could work with the mechanics and the carpenters. He had a fund of humor and was never averse to working on the machine from early in the morning until late at night. For the Voisins, the days of stretching each franc had gone, and no longer was it necessary for their sister to send food parcels from Bourg-en-Bresse. Farman and Delagrange in turn were friendly, although Delagrange did feel that he was not getting the same treatment from the Voisin Frères.

By 1907, Voisin had a few other clients, notably a Russian, Prince Chalmiky, and a Dutchman, but neither of the Voisin planes for these two would-be fliers ever got off the ground successfully. Voisin disclaimed all responsibility for the design, and the clients paid their bills, thus helping the financial state of the Voisin factory.

It was different with Henri Farman. He and Voisin managed to work fairly amicably together, and after four months their co-operation, in spite of occasional arguments, resulted in their first machine being wheeled out of the hangar on the morning of October 7, 1907. In spite of a thick ground mist, Farman took the machine into the air without any difficulties or problematic snags. Everyone cheered as it rose from the ground. Farman's skill in flying the Voisin-Farman machine was apparent from the first. Within a month he was able to fly almost three quarters of a mile, much to the delight of the workers in the Voisin factory who had worked so hard to make those flights a success. Delagrange was not so happy. He had a similar machine, but there were days when he could not get it off the ground.

By the end of 1907 Farman held the French long-distance record, which he had made on November 9, when he won the Archdeacon prize for the first official recorded flight of 150 meters—about 450 feet. He surprised everyone that day by flying almost 3,400 feet and staying in the air for an hour and a quarter. It was the first time in France that any machine had stayed in the air for longer than a few minutes.

The year 1908 began with a great triumph for both Farman and Voisin. On January 13, 1908, nineteen months before the Reims meeting, Henri Farman made his attempt on the Deutsch-Archdeacon prize of 50,000 francs for one closed circuit of one kilometer. Farman's hangar had been built at Issy-les-Moulineaux, a suburb southwest of Paris. It had been a military ground which, by his influence, Ernest Archdeacon had managed to lease for his flying experiments. There were few places which Archdeacon could not enter or use if he felt it would help aeronautics.

Voisin had built two hangars at Issy, one for Delagrange and an identical one for Farman. There was a friendly competitive atmosphere between these two—both wanted to win the Deutsche-Archdeacon prize, not for the money award but for the prestige that would go with it. In fact, Voisin later stated that Delagrange had offered to give him the 50,000 francs if Voisin would give him preference in the assignment of their small staff. But Voisin had other fliers to watch, all trying to win this prize. Blériot, Pischof, and Esnault-Pelterie were all making preparation for an early attempt on the short but difficult task of flying in a circle for 1 kilometer, and Farman was the better pilot.

Henri Farman solved the problem. While Delagrange argued with Voisin, Farman informed the officials of the French Aero Club, the judges for the prize, that he was ready for the attempt. Giving Voisin little notice, he had his machine taken into the field and waited for the judges to take their places. It was a great day for Farman, and even Gabriel Voisin shared his optimism, for he had built the plane and claimed its design as his own.

The circuit was well marked, a pylon, 500 meters away, being the turning point, while the wind was enough to keep any early mist from settling. The circuit course was measured and agreed, and the judges stood by with stopwatches in their hands as Farman climbed into his seat and a mechanic took hold of the propeller. A hand signal, a wave from Farman, and the propeller was swung. The engine started instantly, and the man leaped back, to safety. Gathering speed, Farman took the machine slowly across the field until with a surprisingly short run, he lifted it off the ground. Moments later he was crossing the starting line and on his way. Farman gained height, increased his speed, and dipped slightly into his first turn. He rounded the pylon and circled for the second turn without losing speed. He banked again into the full circle and slowly dropped back to earth again.

When Farman made that first circular flight, he was almost thirty-seven, whereas Gabriel Voisin was only twenty-seven and his brother Charles two years younger still. Louis Blériot was a few months younger than Farman, and Delagrange about the same age.

Farman landed from his circular flight with an ease that surprised everyone. His success made everyone cheer for the sheer joy of seeing such a perfect flight. For the first time in European flying history a pilot had flown a circle, and even if he had been in the air for only 1 minute 28 seconds, it was something no one had ever before succeeded in doing. The 50,000 francs was not the real objective— it was only the inducement to try—but the prestige was insuperable. As would be expected in the months to follow, circular flights were so commonplace that they passed unnoticed. Such was the rapid progress then being made.

The Farman-Voisin plane used that day was, in spite of Voisin's subsequent protestations, the result of their dual enterprise. Farman had attended to the power end: the engine, the shape and position of the gasoline tank, the radiator and its location, and finally the design of the propeller. The Farman-Voisin machine had two wheels under the front wings and two smaller wheels on each of the tail wings and rudder unit. The rudder was worked by cables from the pilot's seat in the middle of the wings. There was a short elevator plane in front and a little above the pilot. Ailerons had not been perfected at that time, although Esnault-Pelterie had tried them on one of his gliders. Fortunately Voisin's design of wing planes gave firm stability even in crosswinds. The two wings were about thirty-three feet in span and almost five feet apart. Measured from front to back, the wings had a depth of six and a half feet, and the plane weighed, when on the field, a little over 1,000 pounds. The wings were made of spruce and pine, as were the struts, which had cross-bracing wires to strengthen the machine.

Farman had decided on an Antoinette V-8-cylinder engine, about 40 to 50 horsepower. This unit weighed only 154 pounds. In those days there were only two engines fit for aircraft; Levavasseur's Antoinette, originally made for motorboats, and the Anzani, a 3-cylinder unit, about 25 horsepower, which at the time was being used by Blériot in his monoplane. The Antoinette engine speed was 1,100 r.p.m., whereas the Anzani was nearer 1,500 r.p.m. There was one interesting feature about Levavasseur's engine—he used direct gasoline injection instead of injection through a carburetor. It was water-cooled by evaporation, the water being turned into steam and condensed for recooling. The Anzani was much lighter than the Antoinette, weighing only 65 pounds, as it was air-cooled. These two Frenchmen, Anzani and Levavasseur, gave France an undoubted lead over all other European countries. By the time the Reims meeting was over, several other engines were being marketed.

The only disappointed man the day Farman made his first circular flight was Léon Delagrange. He had often been disgruntled with Gabriel Voisin, who had many times favored Farman by giving him preferential treatment, but when Voisin needed money, it was always to Delagrange that he went. Strangely, when Voisin had money, he was never around to help the artist-flier, or so it seemed to Delagrange. Yet he was faithful to the Voisins and stayed with them until Blériot flew the Channel, when he began to prefer the monoplane to the biplane. Somehow it appealed more to his artistic mind, though he realized that while he may be a successful artist, he would never quite reach the top rank of fliers.

What kept Delagrange in flying circles was his desire to mix with the more famous fliers, attend Aero Club dinners, and be welcomed in that social circle. He seemed to accept rebuffs as long as he could be seen to be one of the competitors whose name appeared from time to time in the press and society columns. At one time he had a keen desire to design his own planes but was soon talked out of that by the more practical-minded Gabriel Voisin who, although much younger, knew more about flying at twenty than Delagrange would ever know.

When Reims Week opened two and a half years later, Delagrange was still occasionally flying Voisin-built planes, not too successfully as far as the money prizes were concerned, but at least with the satisfaction that he was there as a competitor. His best flight before Reims was a cross-country one of eleven miles. It was one of the longest flights by a Frenchman at that time, but thereafter he slipped slowly out of sight and little was heard of him in the great influx of new faces and new names following his subsequent failures of 1909.

Not so Henri Farman. Always the equal if not the superior of Voisin, he never allowed either of the brothers to fly any of his planes, at least not when he was around. He paid well, but he expected results. After the celebrated circular 1-kilometer success in the Deutsch-Archdeacon competition, he ordered another plane from Voisin with many features which he felt were necessary. Voisin, very enthusiastic, complied with Farman's requirements. During October Farman fitted ailerons, the first practical ones that could be controlled with ease. His flights had always been modest, at safe heights and within close view of the airfield, but now, with ailerons, he flew across country and became the first airman to fly from one city to another—Bouy to Reims. On the next day, October 31, 1908, he created a new French altitude record of 82 feet.

It was Farman's mechanical skill and natural talents for flying that enabled him to maintain his lead over most

of the world's fliers at that time. His successes in 1908 influenced him to make another plane, which he called the
Henri Farman No. 2, something far ahead of anything
that had yet flown. It was superior to the Wright plane
which Wilbur had demonstrated for the first time in France
the year before. Farman patiently supervised the construction, choosing the engine and regaling his friends with the
many records he would break and the prestige he would
gain.

At last his Farman No. 2 was finished. One can imagine
his optimistic feelings when he arrived at the Voisin works
to take delivery, always a very formal occasion. But Gabriel
Voisin was not there, nor was his brother, Charles; no
one seemed to know anything. It was obvious to Farman
that something was wrong, really wrong. He soon learned
what had happened. Gabriel Voisin had sold the plane,
designed and built through their dual efforts, to an Englishman, J. T. C. Moore-Brabazon, later Lord Brabazon of
Tara, and holder of the first pilot certificate issued by
the British Aero Club. Moore-Brabazon crashed this plane
the following May, but on the day when Henri Farman
learned of Gabriel Voisin's action, he could not control
himself any longer.

Always a difficult, vacillating individual, Gabriel Voisin
had, this time, gone too far. Farman sat down and then
and there canceled his orders. "If I can't trust you," he
told Gabriel, "I will not work with you. I will make my
own planes and you can make yours. I will have my own
factory."

In this irate frame of mind Henri Farman, with his
brother Maurice, opened his own works at Châlons, an act
which proved fortuitous to them and tragic to the Voisins.

As Farman said later after flying so well at Reims, "Voisin's action gave me the opportunity I had been uncon-

sciously seeking. Now I have my own works, I am independent of anyone, and I have more orders than I can
fill."

He showed his independence when he built his first
plane, the Farman No. 3. It retained many features of the
Voisin-Farman No. 2. He kept the tail assembly and the
50-horsepower Vivinus engine. His ailerons were easily
controlled, and the tail plane assembly, if anything, proved
better than his previous model. He first flew it on April 6,
1909, and during that summer flew it successfully many
more times. By August, looking ahead to the Reims meeting which, he determined, would bring him added fame, he
made several changes—opening the tail unit to give it two
rudders and a change of engine. This time he used the new
Gnome rotary engine—50 horsepower—which was proving very successful in other planes.

Henri Farman's No. 3 was quick in takeoff and easy to
land. As one newspaper reported, "The Farman came to
earth with the least shock, even when he had passengers
aboard." His wheels and skid were an improvement which
many later copied to ensure a smooth landing instead of the
series of hops and bumps which most had to endure. When
he appeared at Reims, Farman had confidence. His machines, like himself, were well known, and by the Friday
of that celebrated week, he was ready for the great challenge, the Grand Prix de la Champagne.

He took off, knowing he had to stay in the air until
twilight, the official hour of closing, to make his final
claim to fame and the prize that went with it. He flew
circuit after circuit, out beyond the racecourse, back again,
and off once more into the country. Exposed to the cold
air and the full force of the wind beating against him,
Farman flew on. Cold and numb, unable to move more
than a few inches, never daring to let his control relax, he

stayed up with a determination that only those who have
sat in the open cockpit of those old planes can realize. He
passed Comte de Lambert's best time, Paulhan and Tissandier's records were broken, and only Latham's record
remained when, with three quarters of an hour before
darkness was due, Farman made that all-important circuit
to beat Latham's 154 kilometers.

Still not satisfied, as long as he had gasoline in the tank,
he refused to come down. The judges were putting their
watches away as the day's official flying was almost over—
but Farman continued. The light was fading, but he flew
over the racecourse once again until his engine spluttered
and then finally stopped. After his usual perfect landing,
Henri Farman, cheered by all those who had stayed to see
his wonderful performance, was helped from his machine,
cold and stiff but elated with success. He had proved himself capable of building a good reliable plane, and with
180 kilometers officially credited to him, after 3 hours 5
minutes of intense flying, Henri Farman had won the Grand
Prix he so desperately sought and with it the prize of
50,000 francs. It certainly had been "Farman's day."

Farman's times from 70 kilometers onward were:

Kilometers	Time(hrs.)
70	1:11:35.4
80	1:21:38.4
90	1:31:45.6
100	1:41:47.2
120	2:02:31.2
130	2:12:46.2
160	2:43:35.4
180	3:04:56.4

When it was over, Farman had little to say. "I have been
very lucky today," he told a crowded hangar. "My new

engine was wonderful, it brought me good luck. I had nothing but trouble with the old engine. Every day it gave me trouble. Now I am very happy."

"Weren't you cold?" someone asked.

"Cold," he replied, "I was almost frozen. I had put on three woolen jackets, one over the other, and two pairs of socks. I was still cold, but I dared not stop. I had to keep going as long as the engine kept going. The engine ran better at a lower altitude so I kept as low as I dared. I had only sixty-three liters of gasoline but I was determined to stay up until it had all gone. My luck has turned and I have won the only race I really wanted to win."

The Seventh Day

Saturday's program was sure to attract the greatest crowd of the week. The newspapers had been increasing their tempo. The *pièce de résistance* would be the Gordon Bennett Trophy for which everyone had been waiting. Speed fascinates. Motor racing thrills had now given place to airplane racing, and by early morning all roads led to Bétheny. Nobody could talk of anything else—they had been waiting for this one event and, with it, as an hors d'oeuvre, the Prix de Tour de Piste—one lap of 10 kilometers—for the fastest pilot.

There was no wind, only a light breeze. The sun rose in a clear sky to give a warm sunny morning that gave promise of good flying under ideal conditions. As one man said, "After the bad weather at the beginning of the week, the 'aerial gods' are being kind at last." By ten o'clock all the machines scheduled to take part in the speed races were out of their sheds and on the field. They were a wonderful sight to newcomers, those that had not been able to get to Bétheny during the week. The parking area was packed, and the low barriers were jammed with visitors. There were no seats vacant in the grandstands. Many people had brought chairs onto the restricted areas in front of the enclosures and were arguing with the gendarmes for the right to remain.

Many planes had already been up, to test their engines and "feel" the conditions above the ground. Curtiss, the lone American, was out early. He was not taking any chances, and during the early morning, he worked with his mechanics testing every wire, tightening every nut, and missing nothing in his scrutiny.

The official day began at ten o'clock, and Curtiss waited impatiently for the judges to order the start. A feeling of excitement and tense anticipation filled the stands. Would the Gordon Bennett Trophy go to the United States or be won for France? There were two favorites, Glenn Curtiss and Louis Blériot. No other pilots had their reputation for speed. Curtiss and Blériot had flown so much faster than any others that it seemed certain, barring accidents, that the trophy would go to one of these two fliers.

Glenn Curtiss had the smallest biplane at the meeting. His machine had a wingspan of about thirty feet compared to the Wrights' span of forty feet. The Curtiss plane was a pusher type, which he had built at Hammondsport, New York. It stood out from the others, a brilliant golden color due to the yellow varnish with which he had painted the fabric. He called it *The Golden Flyer*. It was similar to an earlier plane, *The Gold Bug,* which had been covered with a golden-colored balloon silk.

The Golden Flyer had never been in the air before it arrived at Reims. It had been assembled at Reims, and even the 8-cylinder engine, wihch had been made at Hammondsport, had only been run on the test bench there; Curtiss had installed the engine in *The Golden Flyer* for the first time during the previous week. Always prepared to take a risk, Curtiss gambled with the success of the plane's design and workmanship, and had flown the plane for the first time only a few days before the meeting was officially opened.

Curtiss was sincere and frank when he told the organizers, "I have only one airplane and one motor. If I smash either of these, it will be all over with America's chances in the International Cup Race."

He dare not take risks now. From the very first day he had carefully nursed *The Golden Flyer* and tested its performance. He had waited all that week to concentrate on the speed prizes. With his one solitary racing plane he had only one objective in view, the Gordon Bennett Trophy. If he landed badly, if he crashed, if he had engine trouble or found the controls difficult to operate, he would be finished. So far all had gone well, and now on this Saturday morning he concentrated on the task before him.

While several other planes were being prepared for the day's flying, Glenn Curtiss had already notified the judges he was ready for an attempt on the shorter event, the Tour de Piste. This meant flying for one circuit only. The single circuit would give him a feel of the conditions, as he put it, and be a preliminary for the longer and more important race, the Gordon Bennett. By ten o'clock his machine was on the field, with the racecourse crowded with excited spectators. At ten-thirty Curtiss rose from the ground. His engine was working perfectly, conditions were ideal, as he made his first turn. Banking sharply, he headed for the other end of the field. It was a stupendous effort, and he flashed past the judges' box with a record of 7 minutes 55.4 seconds, the first time anyone had flown 10 kilometers in less than 8 minutes. Elated and satisfied that he could better that and beat any time that Blériot could make, Curtiss made up his mind to go all out for the prize he had come so far to win.

The conditions for racing that day had been agreed. Each contestant would be allowed a preliminary flight which, as in Curtiss's case, would be the lesser important Tour de Piste, and flying would be continued until six o'clock if necessary. Only one attempt would be allowed each contestant, and he would have to declare his intentions before taking off. Curtiss had, he felt, only one real opponent, Louis Blériot, France's hero.

Curtiss described his morning's flight with graphic detail. "After my preliminary flight, when I broke the course record, I realized that the flying conditions were now perfect for the pilot. The sun was shining, there was no wind, not even a breeze. Yet the sun's heat was creating turbulent conditions in what had been called the backstretch.

"The previous day the backstretch of the course had given some trouble to the fliers and in the early afternoon had been dangerous. More than one had crashed, though without injury to anyone. It was only a few hundred yards, but it had to be flown with great care. It could not be avoided.

"I knew it could get worse," Curtiss said, "so we hurriedly refilled the gasoline tank, gave the machine a final checking, and spun the propeller. Being far back from the takeoff line, I got the machine quickly off the ground and climbed as high as I could before passing the judges' stand below me. With the nose of the machine pointing down sufficiently to gain more speed, I headed for the far end of the field. The throttle was wide open, it was my only chance. I banked steeply as I turned toward the 'rough' part of the course.

"The air was wild. It seemed to be tearing at the wings.

It pitched and rolled, but my speed gave me that little extra stability I needed. Seconds later I was through it, but I made up my mind to avoid it on the next lap. Banking sharply at the turns, there was nothing else now but to keep the throttle fully open and head for the final turn. It was all or nothing."

Curtiss landed to a tumultuous reception which increased when his time for the two circuits was announced —15 minutes 50.6 seconds. He had flown three successive circuits, each well under 8 minutes. No such flying had been seen before. If Blériot could beat that, he would have to be a super-flier, even with his highly powered machine.

Curtiss watched his mechanics wheel his golden-hued plane back into the hangar. He had made his effort, and the machine had come through with satisfaction. There was nothing to do but to watch the others, with only one to fear, Blériot.

Others followed. Cockburn, from England, took up his Farman, but the heavy wide-span biplane was no match for the conditions. He made one lap, then gave up after passing through the dangerous backstretch. Lefebvre was next, the first Frenchman to fly: he was serious and grim; no stunting and no exhibitions of steep banks were allowed. He stayed up for the full course, but his time was almost 21 minutes, a hopeless effort, but the best he could do in his French-made Wright. Flying then stopped for the luncheon interval.

Latham was first to get under way in the afternoon. He was still hopeful of recovering the prestige he had lost over his failure to fly the Channel and being left behind when Blériot took off while he was still asleep. Now his Antoinette was in good trim, and he had been recording some fast times. His first circuit was fast, but on his second lap he struck the "turbulence" that almost upset Curtiss. It was too much for his larger plane, and he failed by two minutes. Blériot was now the only one who could keep the trophy for France.

The excitement was now intense. Blériot was climbing into his seat. All morning and part of the afternoon Blériot's team of mechanics had been testing and checking his fastest machine. It was larger than either Curtiss's or Latham's, and it had been fitted with a new powerful 80-horsepower 8-cylinder water-cooled engine with a chain-driven propeller. In the first trial the plane had given him a terrific burst of speed. It seemed impossible for him to lose.

The crowd watched with tense feelings as the monoplane rose higher, gathering speed as it flew toward the stands. It was still climbing as it passed the judges' box. Then it leveled out, and with its powerful engine roaring, the on-lookers saw it heading toward the far end of the racecourse where it would turn. Would Blériot beat Curtiss? was all they thought as they watched him receding from their view. He banked sharply as he made the turn and quickly vanished into the haze. Those with field glasses were more fortunate, as they could still see the monoplane banking toward the longer leg of the circuit.

Blériot cleared the pylon with little to spare. He straightened his machine and flew on, bringing those in the grandstands to their feet. The cheering was spontaneous as the word passed—Blériot was easily beating Curtiss's record time. They were still cheering when the monoplane again headed for the distant marker. The first lap was over. The judges' time for Blériot's first lap was a startling 7 minutes 53.2 seconds—4 seconds less than Curtiss's first lap. Someone shouted, "Another circuit like that and he'll win."

As Blériot flew on in magnificent style, Curtiss watched with mixed feelings from the back seat of a fellow American's car. Obsessed with the one desire to win the Gordon Bennett Race, yet unable not to admire the Frenchman's wonderful effort and his expert handling of the monoplane, Curtiss resigned himself to losing the race.

As he watched, Curtiss could see Blériot heading toward the danger area of turbulence, the spot he had managed to avoid on his last lap. But the crowd was unaware of that as they stood there still cheering with excitement, urging Blériot on toward the finishing post and success. For a moment the monoplane fluttered, swinging a little to one side unnoticed by the excited spectators; all they saw was Blériot making his last turn, banking toward the final marker. But Curtiss turned away. As far as he was concerned, the race was over—Blériot was coming in to land. He saw him skimming over the ground, still a few feet in the air, until, dropping slowly beyond the pylon, the monoplane bumped its way to rest.

Blériot stood up to acknowledge the ovation. The more they cheered, the more Curtiss reacted. He shrugged his shoulders—his 15 minutes 5.6 seconds was not going to be good enough; Blériot was a certain winner. Curtiss sat in the car; there was nothing else to do now but wait for the inevitable. He still had another day, when the Prix de la Vitesse and the Tour de Piste, both speed races, would be decided.

The shouting stopped. Its suddenness was uncanny, so unexpected that for a few moments Curtiss sat dazed. A man nearby gasped as he pointed to the flagstaff at Curtiss's back where the American flag was being hoisted to the masthead. Curtiss looked dully at the Stars and Stripes fluttering in the breeze, unable to believe his eyes. Then someone shouted and rushed toward him waving his hands madly. It was Cortlandt Bishop, who had been to the judges' box.

"You win," he shouted. "You've beaten him by almost six seconds."

At half past five, with another event still scheduled, the Prix des Passagers, the stands and reserved enclosures were still full of spectators. The depressed feeling following Blériot's defeat was soon forgotten, and although there were only two competitors, Lefebvre and Farman, there was no lack of interest.

Farman was quickly in the air. He had to fly the 10-kilometer circuit with at least one passenger, and he completed the course in 9 minutes 52.8 seconds.

Lefebvre took off as Farman landed, but his time with one passenger was 10 minutes 39 seconds. Farman, intent on improving his status as an all-round pilot, went up again and was warmly applauded when, with two passengers, he passed over the line in the same time as Lefebvre with only one passenger. The additional weight was 292 pounds, a load which many would have found impossible to take into the air at all, let alone fly 10 kilometers without incident. The prize of 10,000 francs was well earned.

When most of the crowd were thinking of leaving, they had a pleasant surprise which restored any dejected feeling: Blériot was bringing out his machine again. This time, to their surprise, the signal flags informed them that he was trying for the single-lap speed race—the Prix de Tour de Piste—worth 7,000 francs to the winner. The turbulent spot was calm in the evening air, and Blériot quickly showed them that his first flight in the Gordon Bennett Race was no fluke. 7 minutes 47.8 seconds later, he crossed the line, having beaten Curtiss's time of 7 minutes 55.4 seconds; Blériot's time was never bettered at Reims.

By the time the excitement died down the twilight was beginning to cast evening shadows across the ground, leaving only one more day to end the Reims Week. It would be an anticlimax, but at least it would give many an opportunity to see these famous fliers before they went home.

Saturday, August 28, had given them a day of wonderful flying and put Glenn Curtiss in the top class, if only by six seconds, yet as someone exclaimed, "You can go a long way in six seconds especially when you are flying." He had given them a wonderful demonstration of flying, unsurpassed by anyone at the meeting.

Glenn Curtiss was born in Hammondsport, a small town in the grape belt of New York State. He was one of the few persons in the world's aviation history who returned to his birthplace, started a business there, and created an industry that was to achieve international fame. As a young boy he worked in the vineyard his grandfather had planted. He came back from time to time, riding a bicycle, to see his grandmother and later to open a bicycle repair shop with the aid of the local druggist. It was not long before he was selling bicycles so well that he could employ a manager and open a second bicycle store in another town nearby. In his spare time, he took to bicycle racing for recreation.

In this way, Glenn Curtiss's early life followed that of the Wright brothers. He was twenty-one when he married and realized he now had to work harder and look to other fields to conquer. He decided, as had the Wrights a few years earlier, to make his own bicycles, which could be sold for four or five times the cost of manufacture; in this, he was helped by a local banker. Before long he had progressed, like the Wrights, into making a motorcycle.

Eugène Lefebvre at the controls of his Wright biplane *(Musée de l'Air)*

Eugène Lefebvre banking on turn *(Musée de l'Air)*

Anzani engine, the type used by Louis Blériot to cross the English Channel *(Science Museum)*

Rotary Gnome engine with metal propeller *(Musée de l'Air)*

Henri Farman winning the Deutsch-Archdeacon Prize, 1908
(Smithsonian Institution)

Henri Farman in his biplane *(Musée de l'Air)*

Henri Farman flying his biplane *(Brown Brothers)*

Glenn Curtiss in his *Silver Dart* over the frozen Lake Bras d'Or, February 23, 1909, the first flight in Canada *(Smithsonian Institution)*

Glenn Curtiss flying *Gold Bug,* 1909 *(Smithsonian Institution)*

Glenn Curtiss hangar at Reims *(Musée de l'Air)*

Glenn Curtiss at the controls of his biplane *(Musée de l'Air)*

Glenn Curtiss flying at Atlantic City, 1911 *(Library of Congress)*

Léon Levavasseur (left) and Henri Latham at Reims *(Musée de l'Air)*

Louis Paulhan's crash at Reims *(Musée de l'Air)*

Louis Paulhan making his record flight over Los Angeles, 1910
(Library of Congress)

Henri Latham flying his Antoinette at Reims *(Musée de l'Air)*

Henri Latham in his Antoinette *(Royal Aero Club)*

Louis Paulhan's Voisin biplane flying near the grandstands
(Musée de l'Air)

Blériot crash at Reims *(Musée de l'Air)*

Henri Latham's plane being hauled into position *(Musée de l'Air)*

Bréguet biplane, 1909 *(Musée de l'Air)*

Bréguet crash at Reims *(Musée de l'Air)*

Léon Delagrange flying Blériot monoplane at Reims *(Musée de l'Air)*

Claude Grahame-White starting his Farman biplane at Belmont Park, New York, 1910 *(Library of Congress)*

Knowing next to nothing about the mechanics of a gasoline engine in 1902, he decided to buy the parts and build his own. With castings bought through an advertisement, utilizing parts that could be assembled in the rear of his bicycle shop, he finally, some weeks later, fitted the amateurish unit to a bicycle and wheeled it into the road outside. To the amusement of his friends and to his own consternation, the engine suddenly started. Before he realized what had happened, he was heading for the local lake or some trees on the lake shore. He chose the trees.

It was not long before Glenn Curtiss with local backing was able to start his own motorcycle factory, and from that time on the G. H. Curtiss Manufacturing Company was in business. Here his preliminary business life differed from that of Wilbur and Orville Wright. In a sense his life followed that of Henri Farman in that he became interested in flying through racing and not through the desire to emulate bird flight, as had the Wrights when they first met Chanute and read of Dr. Samuel Langley's experiments. Yet strangely there was a link, a connection that was soon to bring Curtiss into that small coterie of birdmen which Langley had created.

The "Riddle of Destiny," as Charles Lamb wrote, "brings together surprising personalities, usually through obscure channels." Curtiss came in contact with the Wrights through the dirigible. At first Curtiss was not interested in any form of flying. Dirigibles and balloons were mere fantasies, and the Wright brothers' success at Kitty Hawk was only hearsay as far as he was concerned. Langley was unknown, and so, too, was his assistant, Augustus Herring. Yet all these were to come together through the action of one man, Thomas Scott Baldwin, an aeronaut who, after ballooning around the world, finally decided to build a dirigible. He was more of a showman than a mechanic. His need for a lightweight

engine led him from Los Angeles to Hammondsport, where
he met Glenn Curtiss. After some production delays, Curtiss
supplied Baldwin with a small 5-horsepower 2-cylinder engine which was promptly fitted into Baldwin's airship, *The
California Arrow*. A few weeks later Curtiss supplied him
with a larger engine. Intrigued with this new outlet for his
engines, Curtiss began to study the power requirements of
airships. For two years, this interest increased until in the
fall of 1906 Curtiss went to Dayton, Ohio, at Baldwin's request, and there met Wilbur and Orville Wright.

Destiny was working overtime. The Wrights imbued Curtiss with a desire to learn more about flying. Baldwin moved
his airship building factory to Hammondsport, and this
drew many aeronauts to the small New York town. The
Wrights helped Curtiss improve the airship's propellers, and
Curtiss, in return, offered to build a lightweight engine for
their latest machine. The Wrights ignored his offer. By
1907, Curtiss had begun to expand the engine factory, but
after breaking the world's land record with a speed of 136.3
miles an hour, he realized what prestige can do for the
practical-minded manufacturer. The newspapers called him
the fastest man on earth.

Life was becoming exciting for this onetime country boy.
Keen to extend his engine factory with Baldwin's successes
in the background, Curtiss exhibited his lightweight engine
in the New York Aero Show of 1906. It was here Glenn
Curtiss met Dr. Alexander Graham Bell. Bell had always
been interested in flying and was a close friend of Dr.
Langley's. Dr. Bell wanted a small lightweight engine for a
glider kite he had designed and persuaded Curtiss to co-
operate. With Curtiss too busy to go to Nova Scotia where
Dr. Bell lived, Dr. Bell went to Hammondsport. By July
1907, Curtiss and Dr. Bell had become such good friends
that Curtiss finally did go to Nova Scotia, more for a vaca-

tion than to talk aeronautics. There he met the group of fliers that soon became part of his life and who were influential in forming Glenn Curtiss's decision to devote his extra energies to flying and leave his engine factory for others to manage.

Curtiss's new partners were John McCurdy, a Canadian; Frederick (Casey) Baldwin, no relation of Captain Baldwin of airship fame; and Lieutenant Thomas Selfridge, the first officer of the United States Army to be appointed by President Theodore Roosevelt to help Dr. Bell in these aeronautical experiments. Curtiss came to terms with Dr. Bell and the others, and with financial backing by the Bells, a new association was formed—the Aerial Experiment Association (A.E.A.), with Curtiss as director in charge of experiments, with a salary of $5,000 a year. Baldwin became chief engineer and McCurdy the association's assistant engineer and treasurer. The new company had two offices, one at Dr. Bell's home and the other at Hammondsport, where Curtiss could supervise the construction of the engines and continue to direct his own company's affairs.

By now, Curtiss was fully integrated into the aeronautical scene. As winter approached, Curtiss began experimental work at Hammondsport, and there, through Dr. Bell's knowledge of Octave Chanute's glider, Curtiss began to design a heavier-than-air machine which had been in his mind for some time. A preliminary glider only served to increase his intense desire to make an airplane that could be flown with a Curtiss-made engine.

Here, Dr. Langley's influence still lingered, and their first plane was called Drome No. 1, using Dr. Langley's original nomenclature—"aerodrome." When it was finally finished in 1908, its wing surfaces covered in red silk, it was given the name *Red Wing* and the word "Drome" forgotten. *Red Wing*, a biplane, had a span of 43 feet 4 inches, and its total plane surface was 385 square feet. A kitchen chair was provided for the pilot and placed above the leading edge of the lower wing. Bamboo poles, for flexibility and strength, were used for the main structural design. Fore and aft stability was accomplished by a small tail assembly of about 44 square feet. Steering was effected by the use of a square rudder, part of the tail plane, and controlled by steering ropes operated by the pilot's lever. Lateral control was not included in this first design. The motive power for *Red Wing* was a Curtiss 8-cylinder air-cooled motor of about 25 horsepower.

The only flat area near Hammondsport was the ice-covered Lake Kenka, but the ice was getting thin and was not expected to last. Time was precious, so, with Baldwin and McCurdy, Curtiss supervised *Red Wing*'s maiden flight on March 12, 1908. They drew lots, as did the Wright brothers before them, for the first to fly, and Baldwin was the winner. Curtiss started the engine, and *Red Wing* began to move across the ice. Soon it was in the air, a good six feet above the icy surface, but it had not gone far when the tail plane buckled. Having only a few feet to fall, no great crash occurred, though several struts were broken. Casey was unhurt, but *Red Wing*, which had flown about three hundred feet, needed repairs before it could be flown again. Bamboo and silk were not invulnerable to the hard surface of an ice-covered lake, so the plane was taken back to Hammondsport for repairs. Casey Baldwin's flight, short though it was, made him the third man to fly in the United States and the fourteenth pilot in the world.

The repaired and strengthened *Red Wing* was again ready for flying by March 17, but this time the plane rose only a few feet and then crashed without warning, leaving an unfortunate would-be pilot to crawl from under the wreckage. *Red Wing* was now beyond repair, and it was decided to design another.

It was not long before they realized that the cause of these two failures was lateral control, which was to plague Curtiss for many years and bring him into direct legal confrontations with the Wright brothers. Dr. Bell decided to use wing flaps, which he called ailerons. He was probably not aware that Esnault-Pelterie and Santos-Dumont had already tried this system of lateral control, and neither was Curtiss. Out of the ruins of *Red Wing*, A.E.A. Group built a second biplane, this time with a cotton fabric covering which they varnished to prevent porosity. It was quickly called *White Wing* and fitted with an undercarriage consisting of three wheels. With the Wrights refusing to put wheels onto an undercarriage, *White Wing* was the first plane in America to have wheels on its landing gear. Progress was being made.

White Wing was in many respects identical to *Red Wing*. The ailerons were new, but simple to work. They would be operated by the natural inclination of the pilot to lean to the high side when either wing dropped out of lateral balance. *White Wing* was fitted with a steering wheel, like an automobile, and this Curtiss also used in *The Golden Flyer* he later built for Reims. The rudder was directly controlled from the steering wheels by hempen ropes. It was a simple arrangement that worked, insofar as the rudder was concerned.

On March 13, 1908, *White Wing* was given its first trial; this time Lieutenant Selfridge was to be the pilot. It was his first attempt. Before the plane had gathered enough speed, the flimsy bicycle wheels could not cope with the rough ground over which it had to run, and it collapsed. Luckily for Selfridge only the undercarriage was damaged. Four days later they tried again, but again the problem was the undercarriage, and they began to think that the Wright brothers' skids were stronger and safer. Curtiss persevered and set to work to redesign it. The front wheel attachment was changed, and the fixed wheel replaced with one that could be steered. On May 19 Selfridge got *White Wing* off the ground for two flights and by doing so joined the small but eminent list of world fliers. He was also the first United States Armed Forces officer to pilot a heavier-than-air machine.

May 22, 1908, was a great day for Curtiss. The onetime motorcycle racer, the man who told Wilbur Wright he was not interested in flying, at last sat at the controls of *White Wing* and covered a distance of over 1,000 feet, remaining in the air for nineteen seconds. Thus Glenn Curtiss became the world's sixteenth pilot and truly one of the "early birds." A few days later McCurdy's name was added to the list, but at the same time he crashed in a strong wind and *White Wing* went the same way as *Red Wing* before it. It was now Curtiss's job to build the A.E.A.'s next machine.

Knowing nothing about aeronautics, Curtiss utilized his experience with the two A.E.A. machines and the flights which he and others had made. Dr. Bell's scientific approach to the problem and the constant discussion they had had, gave Curtiss an insight into the problems on hand. Dr. Bell's records and general approach to the designs of *Red Wing* and *White Wing* gave him the finest schooling, which even the Wright brothers could not better. The daily records kept by Lieutenant Selfridge assiduously checked by Dr. Graham Bell himself proved irreproachable and started Curtiss on a career that made world prominence at Reims the following year. The next machine which Curtiss built was the last he would build for the A.E.A., but at that time he could visualize only one plane and that was the one he had now agreed to build.

The Curtiss-designed plane, the third A.E.A. machine, had many improvements over the previous two. The landing gear was greatly strengthened, wooden runners, or skids, were added in case the wheels collapsed, and these were made correspondingly stronger. The balancers at the wing tips were moved to more favorable positions to eliminate the use of the rudder when balancing. The outward appearance of this third plane was enhanced by the color of the varnish used on the surfaces of the fabric covering to make them tight and impervious in flight; the mixture contained turpentine and yellow ocher. The yellow coloring gave it a distinctive appearance, and this color was again used in the machine which Curtiss took to Reims the following year. Dr. Bell thought it reminded him of a June bug, so that became its name. On June 21, a month after *White Wing* crashed, *June Bug* took to the air with Curtiss at the controls.

For the first few days, only preliminary trials were made, but on June 25 Curtiss, now nominated as *June Bug*'s only pilot, made some spectacular flights. Taking advantage of the clear morning, he made several flights, the first being for almost 2,200 feet, which took him forty-one seconds. The biplane responded instantly to the lateral controls, and Curtiss found no difficulty in using the new ailerons on the wing tips. Not satisfied with the first flight, Curtiss went up again later that same day and flew 3,400 feet in 1 minute, keeping at a height of twenty feet above the ground.

A few days later, the Aerial Experimental Association decided to try for the Scientific American Trophy, valued at $2,500. It had been offered the year before, but no one, not even the Wright brothers, had made any attempt to win the prize. Some said it had been offered to make the Wright brothers demonstrate publicly what they claimed to have done in private. Curtiss and his copilots decided it was time for them to show the Wright brothers they had no monopoly on the building and flying of heavier-than-air machines. On July 4, 1908, the officials of the American Aero Club and the *Scientific American* saw Curtiss in *June Bug* fly in a straight line over 5,000 feet—well over the kilometer distance required to win the trophy.

This flight, made with a 40-horsepower Curtiss V-8 engine, proved what Dr. Bell and the A.E.A. had been saying for some time, that the United States could build heavier-than-air machines the equal of anything built in France. That public demonstration was of more value than any claim for private flight. It was not long before Curtiss was demonstrating that he could make a 180-degree turn, putting *June Bug* into a steep bank and using the rudder at the same time. A skeptical press was at last beginning to realize that the secrecy of the Wrights was not helping the public's faith in their claims to fly and that Glenn Curtiss had done more in one afternoon than the two brothers had done in the five years since they flew above the sand dunes at Kitty Hawk. It was not long before Wilbur and Orville came out into the open and took up the challenge by flying not only for a few minutes but for over an hour.

It is significant, then, that at the army trials at Fort Meyer in September not two months later, Orville Wright demonstrated the Wright "Army" plane not before a few officials, but before hundreds of enthusiastic onlookers. On September 17, 1908, these trials ended abruptly when Orville, with Lieutenant Selfridge as a passenger, crashed from a height of fifty feet injuring himself and killing his passenger. Lieutenant Selfridge was the first aerial fatality. It shocked the Army, and the Wright camp was stunned; to the Aerial Experiment Association it meant changes and a breakup of the association.

Mrs. Bell wrote to the remaining partners, Baldwin,

McCurdy, and Curtiss, "I can't get over Tom being taken
. . . yet it is better for him to die flying than as Langley did
[brokenhearted through his much publicized failure]. I am
sorry for you in the breaking of your beautiful association. . . ."

That, to Curtiss, seemed to be the only solution. He left
the A.E.A. and with Augustus Herring—a onetime associ-
ate of Octave Chanute's—formed a new association, the
Herring-Curtiss Company. Its first contract came from the
Aeronautic Society of New York, and Glenn Curtiss offered
an improved duplicate of *June Bug*. It made its first appearance at Morris Park track in the Bronx on June 11,
1909. It was the first commercially built biplane in the
United States, and the Curtiss-Herring partnership was the
first aircraft manufacturing company. Yellow, like *June
Bug*, Curtiss called it *Gold Bug*, and he flew several circuits
in it to the cheers of an excited New York crowd who had
never seen anything like it before.

While *Gold Bug* captivated the New Yorkers, it brought
to Curtiss success and publicity he needed where others
had failed. *Gold Bug* had only a 30-horsepower 4-cylinder
engine and was somewhat smaller than *June Bug*. The New
York Aeronautic Society was satisfied, but the Wright
brothers were not. They started a patent infringement law-
suit that Curtiss at once disputed. While the patent lawyers
were preparing for litigation, the Wright brothers turned
down a request by the Aero Club of America to represent
the United States at the Reims Flying Week. Their refusal
led Cortlandt Bishop and his brother to urge Curtiss to accept and represent his country in their place. At first not
interested, Glenn Curtiss was finally won over by their
insistence.

"I am not a professional aviator," Curtiss told the Aeronautic Society. "I have only one machine and that is not

built for speed. What chance have I against these European fliers?"

With guarantees to cover expenses and knowing the value of success if he could win any trophy at Reims, Curtiss accepted the invitation and prepared for France. He realized that *Gold Bug* was not suitable for speed racing, so with only a few weeks to prepare for the events scheduled, the Herring-Curtiss Company concentrated on building another and faster plane, a more powerful version of *Gold Bug* and far superior to any they had built before. In a frantic race against time, Curtiss and his staff finally completed the Reims racer with only days to spare. The most important unit was its 8-cylinder V-shaped engine of 50 horsepower. Curtiss needed power, reliable power, if he was to enter for speed races. His motorcycling days gave him the answer to that problem.

So at Reims a few weeks later Curtiss reflected happily on the events of the day; Saturday, August 28, had given him a great feeling of satisfaction, and as he later stood by the open hangar door, with the Stars and Stripes draped above him, he felt he could go back to Hammondsport proud of his achievement, to face the Wright brothers and any others who might challenge his hard-won victory. Though flying was over for that day, the Reims meeting was not finished; there was still one more day of flying—with the last speed races and the altitude prize to be settled. Curtiss watched Farman taking off for the last time before darkness. It was a fitting finale, as Farman's passenger was the president of the French Aero Club. In twenty-four hours Farman, Curtiss, and all the others, those successful and those who were not, would be dismantling their machines and preparing for the future and what it might hold in store for them and for aviation.

The Final Day

Sunday, August 29, was the closing day for the Reims meeting. There would be the two speed races: the Prix de la Vitesse, three laps totaling 30 kilometers, and the Prix de Tour de Piste, one circuit of 10 kilometers. The former was worth 10,000 francs to the winner; the latter was 7,000 francs. Louis Blériot had already clocked a very fast 7 minutes 47.8 seconds Tour de Piste and would be declared the winner if Curtiss or another failed to better that time. Blériot wanted to devote all his energies to the longer speed race, which he felt he could win also. He was not worried about anyone else. Latham, like Curtiss, was trying for both events. To add to the interest for this last day, there would be a competition for height, which everyone expected would be won by Farman.

The sky was clear when the sun rose on ideal conditions. Curtiss and Blériot, always early starters, were on the field soon after dawn, checking their planes. Curtiss, with only his *Golden Flyer*, would be trying for the two speed events. Both men were favorites, and both had been fighting for the speed prizes all week. Seconds, even fractions, counted now. Curtiss, as usual, spent the early morning hours checking and testing every part of his machine. Blériot had one advantage: he could choose from several planes. He chose his latest and fastest, the Blériot XII, which had a new and powerful engine of 60 horsepower, 10 horsepower more than Curtiss's *Golden Flyer*.

Curtiss was the first to take off. A shout to the mechanic holding the propeller, a flick of the ignition switch, and the engine roared into action. The men holding down the tail and the two men at the wing tips saw Curtiss wave a hand to signal "release," and as they jumped clear, *The Golden Flyer* moved swiftly away. His first flight was for the Tour de Piste—one circuit—and he needed to fly over 50 miles an hour to win. Clipping turns, he swung round the pylons faster even than his previous day's race for the Gordon Bennett Trophy. He landed and waited anxiously for the judges' timing. It was fast—7 minutes 53.2 seconds —but not fast enough. For all his skill in cutting corners, Blériot's time the previous day was still 1.6 seconds less for the same distance. Curtiss could not fly again for the same race, so he conceded defeat with his usual grim smile, then prepared for the longer race, the Prix de la Vitesse.

When Blériot climbed back into the pilot's seat not long afterward, every eye was on his monoplane No. XII and the mechanics who swarmed around it. The engine started, stuttering and coughing until all cylinders were firing steadily, and the plane moved slowly forward, wings fluttering up and down as it gathered speed. The crowds were cheering, their shouts of delight almost drowning the roar of the engine as Blériot lifted the machine into the air. Blériot had won one race, had been narrowly beaten in another, and now this third and final speed race seemed certain to be his. The American, they had decided, would be beaten again;

Blériot's new plane had more power, and, to end the argument, monoplanes were always faster than biplanes.

Seconds later Blériot passed the stands and was approaching the first turn at full speed, faster than ever before. He banked swiftly into a steep curve, but the plane seemed to flutter, its wings rocked, and it started to dive. Blériot pulled it back, but it stalled and hung momentarily in the air. He tried to force it forward and regain momentum, but the nose went down. Desperately he fought for control, to get it back on an even keel, but before he succeeded the machine hit the ground. As it struck, first the nose, then the wing, there was a flash as the gasoline tank exploded, and moments later Blériot was seen to tumble through the pile of wreckage. Flames shot up, and the frail wooden framework and the pile of inflammable cotton fabric quickly vanished in a mushrooming cloud of black smoke. It was all over in a minute. The fastest machine at Reims was now nothing but a heap of charred wreckage with only the motor remaining as a single unit.

Within seconds the racecourse was alive with people. Officials, photographers, newspaper reporters, gendarmes, mechanics, and an assortment of spectators rushed to the scene. Blériot, burned but not seriously, walked in a daze, unable to realize what had happened. He was lucky to be alive, lucky to be able to walk into the ambulance that was so swiftly on the scene. He had won the Tour de Piste, but having left the Tour de la Vitesse until the final day, he was now forced to abandon his effort. By the time the ambulance reached the first-aid post everyone knew that Blériot could not continue and the Tour de la Vitesse would be left to Curtiss, with only Tissandier and Latham to oppose him.

The rest of the day was an anticlimax. Curtiss determined not to relax but proved how fast his plane could go. Undaunted by a 5 per cent penalty because he had failed to fly the qualifying races the previous Sunday, he amazed everyone with a brillant flight of 23 minutes 29 seconds for the 30 kilometers, with Latham in his Antoinette No. 29 second and Tissandier, flying a Wright, third. Poor Blériot, who had started the week a favorite for all the speed races, with a fleet of monoplanes to aid him in his quest, and was now recovering from the shock of his crash and suffering from burned hands, had won only 7,000 francs, whereas the American, with only one machine, more than three thousand miles away from home, had won 38,000 francs, almost $7,600, and the greatest prize of all, the Gordon Bennett Trophy.

What is one man's loss, the proverb goes, is another man's gain. How true this proved to be, not only for Curtiss but for Hubert Latham. Beaten by Blériot in his attempt to fly the English Channel, Latham soon got his revenge. At Reims, Latham's prize money was second only to Henri Farman's, 42,000 francs—even more than Curtiss. Adjudged second in the Grand Prix, with his 150-kilometer flight, and fourth (to Paulhan) with 111 kilometers, Latham added a valued second in the Tour de la Vitesse. Not content with these achievements, Latham went on to gain more laurels for the Levavasseur-Antoinette by winning the Prix de l'Altitude.

The competition for high flying was the last major event of the week. Four pilots had entered: Latham; Farman, anxious to add one more trophy to his list; Louis Paulhan, who had only one minor success in the Grand Prix; and Rougier, who had long been a Voisin pilot.

The event strained the necks and eyes of the mass of onlookers, as each plane rose higher and higher, circling like eagles preparing for a distant flight. Latham's plane grew smaller and smaller. He made a most impressive flight, soaring upward sometimes out of sight in the sun's glare.

He made altitude history by flying to an official height of 508 feet to beat Farman, who only reached 360 feet. Latham surprised everyone. No one had ever reached that height, and but for his sealed barograph jamming, the world record would have been higher. Latham claimed to have reached 1,200 feet, but this was derisively rejected.

The conditions that day were perfect for breaking records, especially when the inducement of money prizes was added to the desire. The dead calm which prevailed for most of the day was a great change after the earlier stormy weather. The sight of the four daring pilots in such differing types of machine as they ascended was a sight which no one present would ever forget. As they spiraled upward, many were the conjectures on their heights; it was obviously impossible to judge accurately when they were above 100 feet, as only a few had ever seen a flying machine more than 50 or 60 feet above the ground before.

Latham was almost unknown except for his ignominious landing in the sea off Calais a few weeks before. Léon Levavasseur, the fat congenial designer of the Antoinette, was much better known, although more for his racing motorboats than for his elegantly designed airplane. His smiling, confident-looking face had appeared in all the newspapers. His Antoinette engines were being used by many builders of the heavier-than-air machines—Farman, Voisin, Blériot, and others. Now the last day at Reims was bringing both Latham and Levavasseur belated fame.

Levavasseur was one of the most impressive characters at Reims. He was short and somewhat corpulent, always good-humored, with eyes that twinkled happily from under the visor peak of the yachtsman's cap he wore constantly. A jovial, gregarious enthusiast, Levavasseur was a clever engineeer and an artist. At one time he had been a student at the Paris École des Beaux Arts. His artistic nature enabled him to produce not only a lightweight engine but also a graceful-looking monoplane. "A bird doesn't have two pairs of wings," he is said to have remarked when talking about the biplane. Levavasseur's monoplane, which he called the Antoinette, after the daughter of a codirector, had graceful lines, delicately shaped wings, and a slender fuselage. Its birdlike tail assembly gave it, when silhouetted against the sky, the appearance of an eagle soaring. It made Levavasseur a leading member of a fast expanding group of airplane builders.

Levavasseur's friendly, affable nature gave him entry to every shed. He had met Ernest Archdeacon during Archdeacon's early motoring days and through him had met Voisin and become associated with the glider experiments which had so tragically failed on the Seine four years earlier. Soon afterward Levavasseur had met Blériot and the others of that small coterie.

Apart from Farman, there was no one with Levavasseur's engineering ability and knowledge of the internal combustion engine among the pilots and builders, yet unlike Farman, Levavasseur was not a pilot. He had started his industrial career making engines for motorboats, later to be fitted into a Santos-Dumont airship. When Santos-Dumont built his famous 14-bis box-kite biplane and used an Antoinette engine, Levavasseur decided to build aircraft as well. Thus Levavasseur became involved in French powered flight from its very early days. Subsequently he introduced the direct fuel injection engine, an innovation which did not have full recognition for many years.

No one did more for French aviation than Léon Levavasseur in developing the motive power for those early heavier-than-air machines. Flying would have been impossible without such men, their knowledge, foresight, and ambition.

Another man now dimly remembered even by those who

were alive during those summer months of 1909, was the man who made the name "Antoinette" even more famous than its creator. Hubert Latham was determined to take this opportunity to fight for a top place in that still small but growing number of fliers. At Reims, Levavasseur had four pilots and several of his Antoinette monoplanes. Each of his machines had 50-horsepower engines. The Antoinette engine was becoming one of the most reliable in France. Designed with 8 cylinders, V-type and water-cooled, Levavasseur had developed his direct fuel injection system with surprising success. His Antoinette VII, in which Latham had dived into the English Channel, had been salvaged and rebuilt and became the success of the year, giving Latham many safe flights and winning for him a variety of prizes.

The Antoinette VIII, although satisfactory, was not so successful as the VII. With Latham as chief pilot, this plane became the best known of all, with its double surface wings and aileron-tip control. The weight of the No. VII, with gasoline, was about 1,300 pounds, and it could fly at about 45 miles an hour. Its span was forty-two feet and about thirty-eight feet over-all from propeller to tail. This was not an unusual size, although somewhat larger than the Blériot monoplane flown at Reims, which was only twenty-six feet in span and length. Like most machines in those years, the airframe was built of ash and spruce. These woods, known for strength and lightness, were sufficient for the use to which they were put. They had to withstand a fair amount of shock when landing and severe stresses and strains in the air with contrary winds, air pockets, and gusts which no aerodynamics could envisage at that time. The only satisfactory proof was by trial and error, "more errors and more trials," as Blériot was once heard to remark. That they survived at all was due to the determination of the pilots to stay up and learn by bitter experience what was good and what was bad.

Hubert Latham came of an Anglo-French family. He was an amiable type, with more than enough money to satisfy his desires for sport and similar enjoyment. He, like Santos-Dumont, became fascinated with balloons but unlike Santos-Dumont, never took to airships. Instead, he met Levavasseur and decided to fly the heavier-than-air machine that the conscientious, cheerful builder of motorboats was then designing. He and Levavasseur were soon close friends in spite of the difference in their ages. Their partnership— pilot and designer—never changed, lasting until Hubert Latham's death some years after Reims when he was killed by a wild buffalo on a safari.

Latham flew in France, in England, and later demonstrated the Antoinette monoplane in the United States, flying with much skill over such cities as San Francisco and New York. He took part in the Gordon Bennett Race at Belmont Park the year following Reims.

Latham was instrumental in changing many of Levavasseur's designs, and their planes Nos. VII and VIII were both due to the younger man's keen desire to fly the fastest and most reliable monoplane. He came near to doing this with the No. VII, but the No. VIII was never successful. So, in return, Levavasseur named a later plane *Type Latham*. This machine, in spite of an ingenious design, was not a success, built too quickly to meet an unrealistic delivery date and underpowered with a 50-horsepower motor. The *Type Latham* failed to fly with any satisfaction, even when the smaller engine was replaced with one of twice the power. At one time it was tried with ten wheels— two supporting the tail.

Latham, Farman, and Curtiss were among the few who did not crash at Reims, unlike Blériot who was extremely

unlucky. Although flying every day, they survived the
week and collected most of the prize money. Paulhan had
had his near-collision with Delagrange, but proved to be
one of Voisin's best pilots; he was the oldest in experience
though not in age, having joined Voisin shortly after Farman had severed his connection with the somewhat turbulent builder of cellular box-kite planes. Paulhan's only
reward was the third prize for the Grand Prix, worth
10,000 francs. It was not a great return for all the efforts
he had made or for his spectacular flying, which at times
had thrilled the crowd.

Louis Paulhan's sole flying experience had been gained
with the Voisin biplane. Although flying was for the rich,
he managed to earn enough by demonstrations, and like
Curtiss, with only one machine, he had to be a careful
pilot. At Reims he dare not compete with Lefebvre's spectacular antics. "It is safer," he told his mechanics, "to keep
going steadily than to attempt to put extra stresses and
strains on a machine."

Paulhan acquired a natural instinct for cross-country flying, which offered him great satisfaction. "We must progress, we cannot stay over one field," he told reporters.
"Cities must be linked by air as well as by railroads. We
must show the way."

Paulhan was only twenty-six when he flew at Reims. He
had already completed his military service in a balloon bat-
talion of the French Army, and by the end of an enforced
stay among the "birdmen," as they were called, he became
an enthusiastic pilot. Once out of the Army, he found
work with Édouard Surcouf's "Astra" Balloon Works at
Boulogne-Billancourt. Surcouf, with finances supplied by
Deutsch de la Muerthe, had become well known for his
dirigibles after many years of building the spherical-type
gasbags. Like Santos-Dumont, Surcouf was a unique per-

sonality, designing and building his lighter-than-air dirigibles while supervising all his staff with parental affection.
The result was a family interest that brought loyalty and
enthusiasm from the top mechanic to the poorest-paid
woman who stretched the fabric of the balloon's envelope.
Here Paulhan worked and through Surcouf came in contact with Voisin.

Paulhan's interest in heavier-than-air machines started
with Santos-Dumont when he watched the Brazilian fly his
earliest biplane, which influenced Paulhan to make model
airplanes which he flew successfully. In 1908 he entered one
of his models for the Aero Club of France's Model Airplane Competition. He won it, and his prize was a Voisin
biplane. Unfortunately it had no engine—but this lack of
motive power was a blessing in disguise, making the young
enthusiast all the more eager to make good the deficiency.
He was determined to fly, and that determination urged him
to get others to help him raise money to buy a used engine.
Knowing he dare not fail his friends, he taught himself to
fly and became closely acquainted with Gabriel Voisin in
the process.

Learning the hard way, never taking risks, Paulhan
quickly recognized the benefits of safe, steady flying. He
planned carefully and never left anything to chance. In
many ways he was like Curtiss in temperament—always
careful.

Reims gave Paulhan the opportunity he sought to become a great flier. He had always been influenced by Henri
Farman. As a young man, although flying a Voisin biplane, he had met Farman and spent as much time as he
could watching the older man. He patterned his flights on
Farman's, learning how necessary it was to keep his engine in a running condition and to know how to do a
mechanic's job in an emergency. Reliability was to be an

important word in his vocabulary. It was Farman's influence that helped him in the months following Reims.

One can visualize this young man seeking to gain Farman's unquestioning help when, after the Reims meeting was over, he sold his Voisin biplane and invested in a Farman. It was not long before he added further fame, first in England and then in the United States, by his cross-country flights—often under atrocious weather conditions that forced others to give up.

Six months after Reims, Louis Paulhan went to the United States to gain more experience and win more money prizes. Still resisting all offers to compete in speed races, he nevertheless made a name for himself in the top rank of pilots in a land that boasted such men as the Wright brothers, Curtiss, Lincoln Beachey, Walter Brookins, and Frank Coffyn.

After some short cross-country flights, with little knowledge of the terrain, Paulhan suddenly surprised everyone by flying forty-five miles from Los Angeles to Santa Anita and back, incidentally winning $10,000. It was only eight months after Reims when this Race of the Century, as it was called, made Paulhan a national hero in France and an international flier of note. It demonstrated the risks that fliers had to take in those early days to overcome the dangers involved in flying across unknown country. Aerial maps had not been thought of, but Paulhan's determination showed that such flight was possible. Altogether, his visit to California brought Paulhan almost $20,000 in prize money for endurance flying, a sum not even Farman could better.

In less than a year's flying this young pilot had come from an insignificant model flying competition to rank with the world's best to take many thousands of dollars back to France. The April following Reims was a fabulous month for Paulhan. The Nice Aviation Show had scarcely ended when he astonished the French public by flying across country for 118 miles in a little over three and a half hours. It was a performance in bad weather conditions that set the newspaper reporters aglow with enthusiasm. But Paulhan was only just beginning. Without resting, he set his sights on England and the *Daily Mail* £10,000 prize for a flight from London to Manchester. On Tuesday, April 27, 1910, he and Henri Farman were assembling his biplane at the Hendon Airfield.

As at Reims Louis Paulhan planned his flights with care and precision to an astonishing degree. This little man worked alongside his mechanics, a lesson he had learned from Farman, leaving nothing to chance. Tightening screws, testing the wire stays, checking with serious eyes, he worked while others slept. In this he was encouraged by his petite and charming wife, who followed him on most of his adventures—and to him they were certainly nothing less. He could relax and enjoy the lively company that gathered around them on their travels.

Asked how he managed to keep awake and alert on his long flights over unknown country, Paulhan replied, "I sing aloud . . . it passes the time. I feel better when I sing. I was a soldier once and soldiers love to sing . . . it keeps them going when they are feeling tired and depressed."

The race from London to Manchester was a test for depression. Flying against the Englishman Claude Grahame-White, five years his senior but with no comparable experience, Paulhan planned the flight in detail, allowing nothing to deflect his plans. After supervising the preparations, he was off the ground while the older man was still sleeping. Yet on that race from London to Manchester, the first really authentic cross-country race of 185 miles, from one big city to another, Louis Paulhan took no ad-

vantage of Grahame-White's fatigue. Grahame-White had
been working at great odds to get his plane repaired after
a sudden gale had turned the machine upside down and
broken its back. Paulhan and Grahame-White had promised to give a warning to each other when either would
be taking off. Somehow, in the excitement, the warning
note from Paulhan did not reach Grahame-White until
after Paulhan was in the air. In spite of this, the Englishman lost only seventy-four minutes. Farman, unable to take
sides—both men were flying Farman biplanes—helped
them both, even though their departure points were several
miles apart. There were few expert aircraft workers in
those days, only carpenters and automobile mechanics.

That same afternoon, April 27, 1910, shortly after five,
Paulhan kissed his wife as she pinned a St. Christopher
medal on his coat, and climbed into the plane. Most of
the onlookers thought he was making a test flight until they
saw him circling steadily to gain height, then turn to the
north and to Manchester. The wind, freshening as he rose,
now became squally. It started to rain, which nearly
blinded him as he sat in the open cockpit. Singing did
little to help him. He was cold, his hands holding the
controls were numbed; he wanted to go on, but his body
urged him to go down. He was following the railway line,
and as the visibility lessened toward the evening darkness,
he could see the "special" train which Farman had ordered
from the railway company traveling below. He kept on
flying. He would go as far as he could until he was forced
down by the freezing conditions.

In the meantime, Grahame-White, now awakened,
rushed from his nearby hotel with only one thought: Paulhan's on his way. He had been caught napping in both
meanings of the term. The wind was getting stronger,
gale conditions were predicted, and he was urged to wait

until morning. It would soon be dark; what chance had he to beat Paulhan now? Grahame-White's answer was terse and to the point. "If Paulhan can fly, so can I. The weather is bad for us both, and I'll fly in the darkness to catch up with him."

With little thought of Grahame-White, Paulhan held steadily to his course. He could still see the special train beneath him and a white handkerchief being waved from one of the windows. It was his wife's. At 8 P.M. the light was so bad, he realized it would be wiser to land. The careful Frenchman, true to his cautious nature, looked for a landing field where there were no trees or obstacles. A few minutes later he was on the ground alongside the railway, numbed with the cold, but well on his way. He found himself near the Cathedral City of Lichfield, where Dr. Samuel Johnson was born—with only 48 miles remaining of the 185 miles he had set out to fly. While he was being driven to the city to recover from his ordeal and get some sleep, news came through that Grahame-White had landed 57 miles behind him. It was now dark, and the Englishman was resting in the home of a nearby doctor.

News of Paulhan's landing was quickly flashed to Grahame-White. When he heard that the Frenchman was down at Lichfield and resting in a hotel, he forced himself again into action. With no thought of waiting until dawn, caring little for the risks involved and the dangers of takeoff in the darkness and a flight with only the occasional light from a railway station to guide him on his way, he made up his mind.

He spoke calmly but firmly. "I am going on now. I am going to overtake Paulhan while he sleeps. It's my only chance."

No one had ever before attempted such a flight; night flying was unheard-of. He would never make it, and if he had to land, it was suicidal. But it made no difference to Grahame-White. His mother and sister were there; cyclists were working to generate a meager glow in the floodlights, willing helpers moved the plane to the best position in the field to avoid the telegraph poles that bordered the railway line, with one car leading the way to give the determined flier a direction to follow. To everyone's relief Grahame-White somehow lifted the plane off the ground and into the air. His Gnome engine, which Farman had given the final check the day before, never faltered. He cleared the railway and the telegraph wires and was soon on his way to where Paulhan was resting.

"It was cold up there," he said later. "Damned cold." But he could see the railway as his eyes grew accustomed to the darkness. As the wind increased, he could hardly keep his course. The plane dropped, rose again, tilted and swung. He cursed the wind, but only engine failure would stop him now.

For Paulhan the news that Grahame-White was flying through the night and was only a few miles away came as a bombshell. He was out of his hotel in seconds and hurrying through the darkness toward the field where his plane was being prepared. It was four o'clock, yet the roads around the field were swarming with people: nothing so exciting had ever happened before in this otherwise peaceful countryside. Nine minutes later Paulhan was shouting to his mechanics to swing the propeller and let go the wing tips. With an intense roar Paulhan was once again in the air, intent this time to reach Manchester, if necessary before the dawn broke.

The two men fought their way through the darkness. The rain had stopped, but now the obstacle was the cold wind. They were the first men to fly at night: never before had any airmen dared venture into the air after the first signs of dusk. Yet now, only a few months after Reims, not one but two men raced through the night, intent only on reaching Manchester by dawn. Buffeted by gale-force winds, along an unknown route with only a railway line to guide them, they managed to keep on their course.

Grahame-White was now far behind Paulhan. It was all he could do to hold on to the controls in the wind. The wings of the biplane were almost torn apart in his efforts to retain height and continue to fly. He finally gave up. Five minutes after Louis Paulhan had taken off from the field near Lichfield Grahame-White was bumping along the ground in a field some distance in the rear.

As the Englishman landed, Paulhan was fighting his way toward his goal. No one believed he could get to Manchester, the wind was so fierce and the forecast was for worse. Amazingly he was still flying as the dawn gave him his first sight of the grounds of the suburbs of Manchester. The city was aroused, and thousands flocked to the airfield to cheer him as he landed. Flying that last fifty miles against almost impossible odds was, he said, a nightmare. That he succeeded was a miracle. "I was a fool to have started, but I had to go on" was his only comment as he was welcomed with cognac and hot coffee.

Paulhan's dramatic victory over Grahame-White made him an international hero. Night flying was proved possible through the dogged determination of one man. It had been Reims that had given him the opportunity seldom given to one so young. Competition, as always, was the key to progress, and never had it been so significant in such a short space of time. But Reims had done more: it brought to the world a desire to see more flying machines, structurally stronger, faster, and with more dependable power.

The Other Contenders

After Reims, what next? The end of this remarkable week of flying came too soon for many. There were lessons to be learned, new ideas to be adopted; pilots and airplane builders were looking for new fields to conquer. With the Reims epoch-making air races another contribution to history, what benefits would be accrued from this first and famous aero meeting?

Primarily it was to be a unique spectacle where international pilots would compete in every conceivable type of race—speed, endurance, and height—to attract the world's attention to the city of Reims and the champagne producers of that well-known grape-growing district. Its secondary aim, and the one that the Aero Club of France was principally concerned with, was to promote national, if not international, interest in the growth of a new industry. The organizers were successful in both, as designers and builders of aircraft were given the opportunity of seeing what others were doing. They could learn from their failures and successes, and pilots could gain experience under varying weather conditions. The money prizes brought the best of the limited flying fraternity together, ultimately to produce a heavier-than-air machine which would fly faster, longer, higher, and with greater durability and stability than ever before. In this they not only succeeded but gave untold pleasure to thousands of visitors.

For the first time, flying was seen to be commonplace. Unheard-of speeds were registered, and every day new heights were reached—the world's altitude record had been broken on the final day, and one man had stayed up for over three hours and had flown 112 miles. Reims showed the world one thing that it had not realized: the mechanical power-driven flying machine was further advanced than even the most optimistic aeronautical enthusiast had realized.

Everyone who attended Reims considered the money well spent. It was estimated that over half a million people paid for admission, but that did not take into account the thousands, perhaps hundreds of thousands, who thronged the fields and roads for miles around. Those who attended the last days were lucky to have almost ideal weather conditions, but those brave enthusiasts who were there on opening day and on Tuesday, when the President attended, were well rewarded for their courage. In the sheds, the hangars, each airplane builder had what was, in a sense, a miniature factory. This was particularly true of those like the Farman, Voisin, Wright, and Blériot organizations. Their mechanics had little rest; their work was no sinecure; what with repairs to the framework and new fabric to cover the plane's surfaces, the overhauling and repairs to engines and propellers, work would continue sometimes around the clock, and no day for them meant less than fourteen to sixteen hours.

It was a pity that Orville Wright did not attend the

Reims meeting, even as a spectator. He would have seen competitive aircraft, always useful to a designer, but he felt he could further his company's activities in Europe by staying in Germany that week. Wilbur was in America trying, with little success, to persuade the government to order Wright planes. Wilbur, after his first success in France in 1908, when he gave members of the French Aero Club a demonstration of flying the like of which they had never seen before, had established his factory in Pau in the southwest of France. Here he had a very friendly neighbor, Louis Blériot. Blériot helped the American with advice in his dealings with French authorities. Writing to his old friend Octave Chanute, Wright praised the French for their welcome: "They are making up for lost time, giving so much time and trouble to assist a stranger as they have given me."

While Blériot helped Wilbur Wright set up his new factory at Pau, Archdeacon and Ferber did what they could to smooth out the problems which arose in Wilbur's dealings with French financial interests. Such problems were numerous in those early days of aviation, but co-operation was always forthcoming if those friends could help.

Wilbur Wright stayed in France for many months, demonstrating the advantages of his biplane and the ease with which it could be handled. Blériot became very friendly with Wilbur Wright, and this friendship resulted in an exchange of patents. Wright's patents on wing warping were later used in Blériot's machines, particularly in the planes he took to Reims.

Pau became a center not only for the air industry but also for training young fliers. Several of the pilots who flew at Reims in August 1909 had been trained at Pau by either Wright or Blériot. Hundreds went to Pau to see demonstrations of flying by these two great pilots. Wright's fame was beginning to spread through Europe, and Blériot reaped the benefit of this attraction. Many notable people were there, including King Edward VII of England and the younger King Alfonso of Spain. Both these monarchs wintered in Biarritz, a famous Atlantic beach resort only a few miles away.

While the well-known pilots of Reims went on to a successful career, there were many who dropped out of the public eye through lack of progress, poor recognition, or insufficient capital. Many of the mechanics who worked, but did not fly, at Reims became famous as the years passed, until World War I loomed on the horizon. A few, more enterprising than the rest, succeeded in making a name for themselves in aeronautical history, but others well known at Reims soon left the scene. Lefebvre was killed a few weeks later, and Captain Ferber, who did so much for French aviation, also died a tragic death before the year was out.

Those who succeeded in spite of failures at Reims, Esnault-Pelterie and Bréguet, were perhaps better known, and yet they, too, had a hard struggle. While the big names —Farman, Blériot, Latham, and the rest—got most of the Reims publicity, there were many others there, not so well known, who made important contributions to flying and airplane design. Esnault-Pelterie was perhaps one of the leaders of the lesser known airplane builders and pilots. His career was varied, but never very spectacular, and he never received the recognition due to him. He built his first powered monoplane in 1907.

Robert Esnault-Pelterie, born in 1881, was one of the few very early European aviation enthusiasts with an engineering training. At Reims, his brilliantly red-painted monoplane became, like Curtiss's *Golden Flyer,* an attraction mainly because of its distinguishing color. His planes were listed under the initials *R.E.P.,* as were also the engines which he had designed and built, like Levavasseur who was his contemporary.

Said Esnault-Pelterie on the first day at Reims: "Having made the finest airplane engine, it was only natural that I should make the finest monoplane to match it." That this did not turn out the way he hoped was due to the superior flying of others, who were better pilots.

Many were the arguments raised after Reims. The main disagreement centered on the use of ailerons instead of wing warping to control lateral balance. Santos-Dumont, knowing nothing of the Wrights' claims and subsequent patents for use of pulleys to warp the wings of their bi-planes, was the first to actually use ailerons. These were movable flaps near the wing tips, much the same as those used today. But Santos-Dumont was not the inventor; it was Esnault-Pelterie who first proposed their use, and his idea was to use a combined wing flap for balance and as an elevator. Santos-Dumont fixed ailerons in his cellular box-kite machine and was well satisfied, while others like Curtiss and Farman used them mainly to avoid infringing Wright patents. Curtiss had installed them between the upper and lower plane units.

Esnault-Pelterie's second machine was notable for the use of hydraulic wheel brakes; these were crude from a modern viewpoint and were not installed on all his planes. He was, like Blériot, a pioneer of the monoplane, especially the streamline features he innovated. Esnault-Pelterie's contribution to aviation was of tremendous value to early fliers. Sitting as they did in the open air, perched among a network of wires and struts or within the narrow confines of a canvas-covered fuselage, aviators were certainly in a dangerous position. To prevent the injuries which could occur, Esnault-Pelterie introduced the seat belt—the first safety measure of any kind.

It was unfortunate that only one of the four R.E.P. monoplanes at Reims was able to get off the ground, but this
may have been due to Esnault-Pelterie having injured his
hand and having to rely on less competent mechanics. With
hopeful anticipation the youthful pilot displayed his R.E.P.
first in Paris and then London, but these brought him little
public success. Not for some years after Reims did his luck
change, for this clever engineer to reap the benefit of his
inventive ingenuity. Toward the end of 1909, he increased
the horsepower of his R.E.P. engine and was soon recording speeds of 60 m.p.h. He later used a Gnome engine with
even greater success.

R.E.P., as he was usually called, was twenty-eight when
he went to Reims, one of a small group of flying men who
had been trained as an engineer. While his earlier designs
had been failures, he was soon making a few small but satisfactory flights. Early in 1908 he had flown distances of
2,000 feet. Never daunted by failures, he used his engineering knowledge to make changes which proved advantageous. Like the Wrights and Voisin, he started with gliders
but changed to motive power after designing and building
his own 30/35 horsepower engine.

He was only twenty-three the year after Kitty Hawk when
he built a glider from Chanute's description. Early in his
gliding trials he realized the importance of balancing—it
was this that led to his use of the aileron flap. He did not
like Wright's warping technique—"It was unsafe and uncertain," he declared—and although he worked from a
false premise, he did find a satisfactory solution to the
problem.

He still kept to his wing-tip bicycle wheels and as if this
was not enough, used a wheel beneath the tail plane as
well, even though others were well satisfied with the wooden
skid which the Wrights had introduced. If only to give him

recompense for his earlier failures, it was Esnault-Pelterie's perseverance after Reims that enabled him to persuade the French Air Force, then part of the Army, to use his monoplane prior to World War I. From gliders in 1904 to power planes in 1907 to recognition in 1912, his foresight was so amazing that he soon replaced his interest in airplanes with rockets and space travel.

Esnault-Pelterie was the first airplane builder to use steel tubing for the structural framework. It was an innovation in 1907, which others soon copied. His R.E.P. No. 2 was a better machine than the R.E.P. 1 and was soon showing speeds of over 50 miles an hour, at a height of one hundred feet. In 1909 he was using a balanced rudder, a covered fuselage, and a reduced wing area. During the next four years, until World War I started, R.E.P. monoplanes made some creditable flights, including the principal European Circuit Races of 1910 and 1911. In the years between the two world wars, Esnault-Pelterie slipped out of sight and was soon forgotten.

Among the other lesser known pilots who attempted to fly at Reims, perhaps the most outstanding personality was Louis Bréguet. He and his brother Jacques were two of the most unlucky men at Reims. They started a flying career by making the world's first helicopter in 1907, but unsatisfied with its performance, they turned to the monoplane with little financial backing. They viewed their plane, the Bréguet 1 bis, with an optimism that was not justified by previous performance. Failure only increased their determination to succeed, and while they made several innovations, they could not compete against the faster and better designed planes that appeared on the Bétheny racetrack. Nevertheless, the Bréguets founded one of the most reliable aircraft manufacturing companies in the world which, when World War I started, made a machine that was undoubtedly superior to many other planes in fighting, reconnaissance, and bombing.

The two brothers Bréguet came from a well-known family of clockmakers. They had become interested in gliders in 1905, then turned to helicopters, finally concentrating on building a powered, fixed wing biplane. This had the general appearance of a Farman-Voisin machine. They showed originality in using steel tubes for the longer structural units of the airframe. Some of the wing spars and struts were made of aluminum. The tail unit had twin rudders to add to the box-kite cell effect.

The metal construction doubtless had much to do in preventing a total wreck when the plane crashed at Reims, but it doubtless contributed to the overweight which even the powerful 50-horsepower Antoinette engine could not entirely overcome. Another innovation was the three-bladed metal propeller.

At Reims the Bréguets won no prizes but learned a lot. The initial bad weather was against them, and when their biplane nosed into the ground on the first Sunday, they never recovered from the setback. It was almost the middle of the week before they were able to get off the ground again, and even then they were unable to fly more than 35 miles an hour and seldom higher than ten feet above the ground.

So while the better known pilots flew successfully, Reims did have many failures, especially at the beginning of the week. Bréguet was not the only one unable to get his plane off the ground. At one period on the first day there was an amazing spectacle when several planes could be seen scurrying across the airfield in all directions unable to rise, uncertain where to turn, and missing each other by inches. Often their efforts ended in a noisy crash of collapsing undercarriages, but the majority never lost hope and just kept trying.

French manufacturers had a distinct advantage over the American and British designers. While propellers were varied in several different shapes and materials, from wood to metal, the French had, in 1908 and 1909, more efficient and more powerful engines. The German influence and the great upsurge of motor racing brought to the aviation industry many excellent engines that were light in weight and compact. The French were the first to introduce the rotary engine, and the V-8 design was created to give greater power in the small space available. Efficiency and economy were the two main considerations that dominated every French engineer's outlook during those early years.

Of the lesser known pilots who took part in Reims, few had attained any success prior to August 1909. An exception was Léon Delagrange, but he made little, if any, impact at the meeting. This was doubtless due to his inability to make spectacular flights; yet he was one of the few men who, with Santos-Dumont, Blériot, and Voisin, were flying in 1907.

If Gabriel Voisin had not received financial help from Delagrange when Voisin's partnership with Blériot ended in 1909, it is doubtful if the firm of Voisin Frères could have survived, and the whole future of French aviation might have been drastically changed. Delagrange met Voisin in 1906. The Voisin finances were at their lowest ebb. Money was needed, bills had to be met and wages paid, when Henry Kapferer, who was mainly interested in airships and balloons, brought Voisin and Delagrange together.

Delagrange had some ideas, and Voisin looked at his sketches. Voisin was not impressed; a number of planes attached to a fuselage was the main idea. What did interest

Voisin was the fact that Delagrange had money and was willing to spend it on this "flight of fancy." He satisfied Delagrange and quickly took him to his shed in the rue de la Ferme, which he called his factory or workshop, and showed the Parisian artist what he had done and what he could do for him.

The first Voisin-Delagrange machine was quite different from the design Delagrange had prepared; Voisin had soon talked the artist out of that. Voisin needed money, and he wanted to build flying machines—his flying machine, not a fantasy of Delagrange's artistic creation. Powered with an Antoinette 50-horsepower 8-cylinder engine, the Voisin aircraft was finished in February 1907 when Farman was still selling motorcar accessories.

On March 30, 1907, Delagrange saw the younger Voisin, Charles, take his machine off the ground for a short test flight of sixty yards, remaining aloft for six seconds. Delagrange took delivery of the plane and paid Voisin the balance of the money which the Voisins needed to pay their wages bill and, what was more important, the overdue bill at their hotel.

Delagrange was soon spending most of his time flying. He made his first solo flight on November 5, 1907, two days before Henri Farman succeeded in doing the same. By then, Voisin had two clients, both with money, both keen on flying—but while Farman had a mechanical brain and an instinctive touch for handling the controls, Delagrange had only an artist's conception of what it all meant. He was more interested in flying as a sport and not as a career.

Delagrange was the sixth man in the world to fly, a distinction that went unheralded in the years before Reims. He was, it seems, always overshadowed by Farman. At the end of 1907 the two men were both flying identical planes, but it was Farman's spectacular feat of flying in a circle for the first time that left Delagrange lost in the acclamations that were heaped on his fellow flier. He never regained his earlier place in flying and within a year of Reims was forgotten by the newspapers, who were only interested in popularity and not previous performances.

Reims gave aircraft builders a much needed boost. The competition showed up faults, displayed the fliers' shortcomings, and disclosed weaknesses in a machine's designs, but it also gave the pilots praise for good flying, for careful handling of controls, for daring, and for all the qualities those early fliers disclosed. For instance, the Antoinette was more stable than the other monoplanes, not excluding Blériot's. Once in the air, the Antoinette needed less skill on the part of the pilot. Latham often flew with a nonchalance that others envied. He would take his hands off the controls, stand up and wave his hat, and then settle back in his seat as though sitting down in a comfortable lounge chair. On one occasion when passing over another plane some feet below him Latham got up and looked over the side of his cockpit, as it was later called, to gaze down at the slower competitor he was overhauling.

Another plane that seemed easier to control was the Curtiss biplane. It had extraordinary speed, and Curtiss appeared to fly relaxed and with confidence, unlike many of the others who had to give any movement intense attention. The only other plane that appeared easy to fly was the Voisin, but it had neither speed nor a prominent pilot capable of capitalizing on its inherent advantages.

Curtiss's *Golden Flyer,* unlike the other planes which flew at Reims, was mainly built of Oregon spruce, only the tail and elevator sections being bamboo. The two wings, or decks, as they were sometimes called, were composed of longitudinal frames with ribs of three-ply wood, glued together. Each wing had about twelve ribs. The wings were cambered and covered with rubberized silk stretched tightly over the ribs and structural members. They were "doped" with the now familiar yellow varnish. The wings were strengthened with spruce struts and braced with a specially made cable. The ribs overlapped the rear spar or structural member, and when covered like the wings, formed the trailing edge.

The wheels of the undercarriage had no shock absorbers, but a brake pedal had been fitted in the front of the pilot's seat so that the machine could be brought to an early halt when it touched the ground and the ignition cut off. Two wheels were placed immediately below the wings while a third was positioned on an outrigger some distance in front of the pilot's seat.

Curtiss's power unit consisted of a 4-cylinder water-cooled vertical-type engine and weighed only 107 pounds. The magneto unit weighed an additional 85 pounds. The fuel tank, as small as possible, could hold a little under three gallons of gasoline. The radiator weighed 30 pounds when full, to give a total weight for Curtiss's power plant of only 220 pounds.

His propeller was wood, again of spruce, which he had designed and fabricated at the Hammondsport works. It measured seven feet and was to Curtiss a thing of beauty, not just a propeller. Because of its curious appearance (it had been fabricated from eight pieces), a metal one was offered to him by a French manufacturer. Curtiss tried the metal propeller but preferred his own. This action by the French was indicative of their friendliness and good intentions.

Curtiss's ailerons, the subject of much controversy and litigation with the Wright organization, were, in fact, small wings placed in between the two main planes. There was one aileron at each end. The balancing control was simple.

If the right wing lifted, he moved his body to counteract this tendency and a control operated from the back of the pilot seat to adjust the ailerons to an opposing direction to give lateral control and regain balance.

When the Reims meeting ended, Curtiss, with the prizes he set out to get safely in his pocket, stayed only long enough in Europe to win another speed prize in Italy. His European visit had been well worthwhile. Having conquered land flying, he was now determined to take another step forward in aviation. Word came to him that the United States naval attaché in Paris had sent a favorable report on what he had seen in Reims. "The aeroplane," he reported, "will have a usefulness in naval warfare."

With that helpful comment, Curtiss returned to the United States, intent on converting a Curtiss land biplane to take off and land on the deck of a warship or, if fitted with floats instead of wheels, to take off and return to the surface of the water. For Glenn Curtiss, Reims had been a wonderful success; for his wife, Lena, who had stayed at home, it was a return that meant more separations but a happiness that comes with achievement and progress toward her husband's ideals.

The Other Aeronauts

After the Reims Flying Week was over, international aviation took on a new outlook. Gone were secret trials; the world, at last, was becoming air-minded. Men, and not a few women, were looking at the airplane with a new approach; it gave them a feeling of excitement with the thrill of danger that speed brings, and it brought a new way to enjoy life, if you had the money and the time. Newspapers in Europe and the United States were reporting aerial incidents, however small and insignificant. Anything connected with flying made news for their readers.

In 1910 and 1911 new names and faces were appearing with strange-looking machines—monoplanes, biplanes, and even triplanes. In the United States, particularly, there was a resurgence of flying. Men who had been experimenting in 1907 and 1908 were realizing that France in 1909 had leaped ahead and had become the world's leading country in aeronautics. It was Reims, a fact which is hard to believe, which gave a much needed impetus to those in America and England who were interested in the possibilities of flying as a means of transport, as an industry, as an investment, or as an outlet for their exuberance. Flying could pay handsome prizes and rewards. In 1910 and 1911 many flying exhibitions were being organized. Cities and towns vied with each other to attract anyone who had an airplane and could fly it. To gain publicity, newspaper owners were offering money for cross-country flights.

England, which had once been a leader in aeronautics— with such scientists as Cayley, Pilcher, and Maxim—gave speedy encouragement to those who sought to emulate the Wright brothers, the Voisins, Santos-Dumont, Blériot, and others. It was perhaps Blériot's flight across the English Channel to Dover that gave the British their biggest shock and woke them up to what was happening in the world's flying circles.

The first of the twentieth-century British fliers was Horatio Phillips. Phillips had made many early scientific contributions to aeronautics. He studied, as Chanute had done earlier, the design of hydrofoils and cambered surfaces. He took out patents as far back as 1884 and late 1891 and even attempted to build a vertical takeoff machine in the early 1900s. Using tethered planes, he made steady progress until in the summer of 1907, after many years of near successes and failures, Phillips was at last able to fly his own machine a distance of about 510 feet. This was the first powered flight in England, yet the name of Horatio Phillips is quite forgotten, lost in the maelstrom of events which were occurring in that first decade of flying.

After Phillips, an American, Samuel Franklin Cody, who had been born in 1861, joined the British balloon factory near Aldershot at the beginning of this century. His job was to aid the then director of the Farnborough Royal Engineers Aviation Center, Colonel John E. Capper, in the design of kites and balloons, but it was not long before he realized that the future of flying lay in the heavier-than-air machine. Colonel Capper helped him to overcome the prejudices of the Establishment, and between them they designed a full-sized aircraft which was, in effect, a "glider biplane." It was followed in 1905 and 1906 by the first British flying machine to be fitted with ailerons. In 1907 Cody, now permanently settled in England, built his first powered plane, a biplane, which was given the official title of British Army Aeroplane No. 1. Cody's biplane thus became the first "army flying machine" in the world, some time before the French and United States governments realized its potentialities.

The first officially recorded flight of Cody's biplane was September 29, 1908, when it flew 234 feet. There were other satisfactory test flights during the earlier summer of that year, and on October 16 the same machines flew almost 1,400 feet before crashing in a poor landing. Cody became a British citizen in October 1909 and between then and August 1912 made hundreds of flights, indirectly preparing the British Army for its trials of World War I. His connection with the British Army precluded his appearance at Reims, although many who did take part were younger men of far less flying knowledge and experience. Samuel Cody was undoubtedly Britain's first successful military pilot and an air pioneer. He was killed on August 7, 1912, when his plane broke up while he was flying.

A British kite designer who worked with Cody was Lieutenant John Dunne. In 1907, not long after Santos-Dumont flew for the first time in France and the Voisin brothers were making a name for themselves, Dunne, at thirty-two, was trying out his two efforts, a monoplane and a biplane, in Scotland under great secrecy. Not much is known of these trials, but within a year he was in England flying his D.4, as it was known, in flights of more than one hundred feet. But the Dunne machines were overshadowed by the Cody biplane, and Dunne reluctantly took his D.4 away from Farnborough and soon afterward joined the Short brothers in their flying experiments. While the name Dunne was soon forgotten, the Short brothers became famous, not only in World War I but later in the development of seaplanes.

The Short brothers—Horace, Eustace, and Oswald— came early to the flying scene, all having been balloonists. When Wilbur Wright made his first demonstrations in France in 1908, the three Shorts quickly became Wright licensees. Their entry into the new industry was too late for them to compete at Reims, but during the late summer of 1909 their first Wright biplane became airborne. This, their Short No. 2, was piloted by J. T. C. Moore-Brabazon, the same flying enthusiast who unwittingly broke the Voisin-Farman partnership by buying Farman's machine from Voisin. His flight in a Short-Wright plane took place in September 1909, a month after the Reims meeting ended. In March 1910 the Short No. 3 was fitted with landing wheels and the Wright launching track abandoned.

Two other British pioneers of 1908, neither of whom flew at Reims, were Robert Blackburn, who had been living in Rouen in 1908 when Wilbur Wright first flew there, and Alliott Verdon Roe. Blackburn made several unsuccessful attempts to build and fly his own machine, but although he contributed much knowledge to aviation, he was never really successful until B. C. Hucks, one of England's best pilots in those early days, joined him in 1911.

Verdon Roe's career was quite different. In 1907, when thirty, he surprised Britain by winning one of the earliest *Daily Mail* prizes in a machine similar to the Wright biplane. Roe was a natural-born flier and a man with a wide knowledge of aeronautics. His first flight was made in June

1908, and for the next twelve months he built and flew several machines of his own design. Many of his earlier flights were made with engines ranging from 6 to 9 horsepower, but it was not long before he was using 24-to-35-horsepower engines to get greater motive power. Roe's nonappearance at Reims was due, like so many others, to insufficient finance at a time when he needed all the money he could get to fulfill the contracts he had made. Roe's name will always be associated with the Avro biplane, which became one of the best-known and best-liked biplanes of World War I. It was unfortunate that Roe was not able to compete at Reims.

The Reims Flying Week was directly responsible for bringing two young Britons into aviation. Both had been attracted to flying by the exploits of Blériot, Cody, the Wrights, and others. Both went to Reims, and both subsequently became famous as pilots. They were Claude Grahame-White and Thomas Sopwith. Grahame-White first flew in December 1909 and Sopwith not many months later.

Of all the fliers between 1903 and 1911 none was so colorful, so much adored by the ladies, or so admired by the men, as Claude Grahame-White. His name, from his first entry into British aviation until the beginning of World War I obscured individual personalities, was synonymous with flying. He organized flying races, he attended flying meetings. After opening a flying school at Pau—near to the Wrights and Blériot—he returned to England and did the same at the Brooklands racetrack. Later, he was instrumental in creating the first big flying center in England at Hendon, in London, where weekly flying displays were held. He started the first British Flying School and even rented airplanes to those who were keen to fly.

Grahame-White arrived in Reims on the first day of the

meeting and found Blériot in his airplane hangar on the Bétheny racecourse working in his new Type XII monoplane—a two-seater high-wing machine powered with a 50-horsepower British E.N.V. engine and a chain-driven propeller. Grahame-White was so enthusiastic when he saw it that he immediately arranged with Blériot to buy it, taking delivery after the Reims meeting was over. Grahame-White had known Blériot for some time, having bought Blériot's acetylene head lamps for the cars he sold through his motorcar showrooms in London. His office and showrooms were, incidentally, only a few yards from the showrooms of that historic partnership Rolls-Royce. In 1907, two years after he started in the automobile business, Grahame-White was well established, crossing to Paris regularly.

Grahame-White's active entry into world flying began in Blériot's hangar. After selling expensive automobiles he suddenly found himself surrounded by men who lived in an atmosphere of aeronautics. They talked of planes, they dreamed of new designs, they relived their failures and gloated on their successes. Reims changed Grahame-White as it had changed so many others, and before he left Reims on the first day, he was determined to learn to fly.

At Reims, Grahame-White was introduced to most of the other competing pilots. He had met Farman many times prior to Reims but was now to see in action the fantastic rotary engine, the Gnome, which the Seguin brothers had installed in Farman's latest biplane.

After Reims, when Blériot recovered from the effects of the crash which had left Grahame-White's Blériot XII a mass of embers, the two met again in Paris to discuss the new plane which Blériot promised to deliver as soon as possible. At this time Grahame-White had never flown as a pilot, only as a passenger. He was now determined to learn to fly.

"No lessons, no machine," said Grahame-White. "Let me work in your factory while my plane is being built."

When Blériot refused, Grahame-White retorted, "If you want me to represent the Compagnie Blériot in England, I must work in the factory. I want to know all I can about it. You can teach me to fly at the same time."

After much argument Blériot agreed to teach Grahame-White to fly, and the Englishman's active, international career in aeronautics began, a career that spanned a lifetime of eighty years.

For the next two months Grahame-White worked in Blériot's factory until his monoplane was finished and ready to be flown. Early on the morning of November 6, 1909, the monoplane was wheeled out of the hangar at Issy-les-Moulineaux. Taking advantage of Blériot's absence (he was giving demonstrations of flying), Grahame-White, with the aid of a friend, took the machine for its first trial. To his surprise the 50-horsepower engine was too powerful, and when he opened the throttle, the tether rope broke and the plane was airborne. After traversing the flying field with everybody shouting, he managed to touch down, to the astonishment of the factory staff, who knew he could not fly, having not yet received the promised lessons. His triumph was brief, however: as he landed, he caught one wing tip on the ground and crashed. It ended Grahame-White's first flight, and he walked away realizing it was time he started getting his flying lessons.

Grahame-White named his new Blériot monoplane the *White Eagle*. In January, after the Blériot factory was moved to Pau, he learned to fly under Blériot's instruction. Because dual controls had not been invented, Blériot could only show him what to do while the plane was on the ground. Nevertheless, after his fragmentary instruction, Grahame-White absorbed all he could and was soon able to taxi the *White Eagle* across the field without trouble.

Early one morning in January 1910, less than five months after he had first arrived at the Bétheny racecourse, Grahame-White made his first satisfactory flight and joined the small group of men who could fly a powered plane. For the next few days he regularly took the monoplane off the ground to test its capabilities and now was able to land without accident. In less than a year after Reims, with flying the only joy of his life, Grahame-White opened a flying school and had a fleet of Blériot monoplanes for his own students to use.

Eight months after Grahame-White learned to fly, he surpassed all expectations by winning the 1910 Gordon Bennett Trophy at Belmont Park, New York. This was the race won the previous year by Glenn Curtiss and now competed for annually. Grahame-White's visit to America was sensational. Before returning to England, he took part in many exhibitions in the eastern states, at Boston and elsewhere, winning an astonishing $250,000 in prize money. He broke records wherever he went, attracting the public whenever he appeared. Thought at first to be merely a playboy, Grahame-White surprised everyone by showing his critics that he was also a first-class pilot. He was daring without being reckless; friendly when attending social gatherings, yet aloof when making his flying plans.

The Boston meeting in September 1910 had been planned along similar lines to the Reims meeting of the previous year. There would be contests for speed, duration, distance, and altitude. Flying had been planned for nine days—one more than Reims. The circuit was 1¾ miles, and to make things really exciting there would be a mock bombing of a battleship. To add to this, there would be a prize of $10,000 for the fastest time from Squantum Field, where the meeting was being held, to the Boston Light and back—a circuit of 33 miles. Twenty contestants crowded the hangars and the field. The Wright brothers were there with three planes and their best pilots; Glenn Curtiss was using the Boston meeting to prepare for the Gordon Bennett Race due to be held the following month.

Grahame-White surprised everyone with his versatility. He could fly fast, sometimes in a spectacular way. He could follow a set course across country making his own maps and planning his route. Taking his Blériot monoplane, he not only crossed Boston Harbor, which the others had decided was too dangerous, but continued his demonstration of nonchalant flying by making a second circuit of the Boston Light before returning to Squantum Field. No other flier attempted this double circuit; even Curtiss declined, feeling it was not worthwhile to try to beat this almost fanatical Englishman.

Having flown the 33-mile course in less than forty minutes, to the astonishment of the crowd Grahame-White again took off, and before the day was over he had broken the day's altitude record, beating Walter Brookins of the Wright team by 800 feet. Earlier in the day Grahame-White had beaten Glenn Curtiss's fast time of 6½ minutes for the 5¼-mile speed race by a good margin. It seemed that nothing was sacrosanct to this fantastically energetic and venturesome pilot.

He was still not finished. The battleship bombing was another highlight of the meeting. The American pilots were now being less antagonistic; even Curtiss and Wright were beginning to show less rivalry, focusing their attentions on Grahame-White. Nothing could be kept from the Englishman. When the mock bombing started, he surprised them all by dropping all his bombs, not only on the deck of the warship, but actually sending two "down the funnels" of the wooden replica.

"Another hit by the Englishman . . . and another!" the announcer bellowed in excitement. "The British aviator has done it again!"

"It is just stupendous," exclaimed a naval observer, "quite unbelievable. This man can hit a warship when flying at fifty miles an hour. What can't he do?"

That remark was echoed again and again that week, both on the field and in the homes and hotels of Boston. If any one man had made the Boston meeting a success, it was Claude Grahame-White. But that was not the end. Apart from taking up passengers for short flights of five minutes at $500 a trip, he picked up a leisurely $50,000 for flying at a Massachusetts fair a week or so later, before going on to New York for the Gordon Bennett Race. In spite of his successes, in spite of the tremendous cash prizes he had won, Grahame-White quickly showed his business ability and foresight. After watching the opposition and learning the strength of the French contingent, he made up his mind to win the International Race. He cabled Blériot that he wished to buy his fastest machine, the 100-horsepower monoplane. Time was short—the Gordon Bennett Race was scheduled for only two weeks later. Would Blériot be able to deliver the plane in time?

The 100-horsepower Blériot did arrive in America but only a few days before. It was the first on the field when the day of the race dawned. Like Curtiss at Reims, Grahame-White had not even flown it before the day of the race. He knew nothing of its capabilities, nor of its characteristics. The 14 cylinders of the new Gnome engine gleamed in the early morning sun as the engine spun into full speed. Full of confidence, he opened the throttle and moved swiftly across the ground. Six circuits later he dropped back to earth satisfied, fully conversant with the plane's peculiarities. He waited. The sky was blue, no clouds, no wind; the conditions were perfect. By eight-thirty the racecourse was packed and all roads nearly crowded with excited onlookers.

The Englishman's achievements had preceded him. As he sent the Blériot across the field, the entire crowd was shouting his name. A short run and he was in the air. This was no playboy now, there was no fooling now. He was taking no chances as he flashed over the white line that marked the beginning of the course. Flying only 150 feet above the ground, he clocked 105 seconds for the first lap.

Alfred Leblanc took off as Grahame-White was still flying his eighth lap. Others followed, but now it was clear that only the Frenchman and the Englishman were in the race, with the Frenchman trying desperately to catch his opponent. The slightly shorter wingspan of the Frenchman and his more efficient propeller were giving him an advantage, yet Grahame-White did not hesitate. He knew what was happening—his throttle was wide open and he banked more steeply than ever at the turns. In a frenzy of wild exuberance, Grahame-White completed the twentieth lap and dropped slowly to the ground, skimming it carefully until he came to a stop exactly 1 hour and 1 minute after takeoff. As he climbed out of his seat, numb with cold and stiff from sitting in one position for so long, a shout came from the grandstands: "Leblanc is down. . . . Leblanc has crashed."

It was true. Leblanc, trying to conserve fuel and reduce weight, had overestimated his plane's capabilities, and with three laps to go, the fuel tanks were empty. Out of control, the speeding Blériot monoplane had swerved from the course and had smashed against a telegraph pole. Until that moment Leblanc was winning easily. Luckily he was thrown clear, uninjured apart from cuts on the face and body.

The rest of the day's flying was an anticlimax. There were more accidents: Brookins was injured and Latham was forced to retire after fifteen laps when he swerved badly and almost crashed into the grandstand. So, with John Moisant beating Alec Ogilvie for second place, the much heralded 1910 Gordon Bennett Race was over. It was Great Britain's first big international win, a shock for the French, who were bursting with superiority, and a disappointment to the American public, who did not expect their fliers to lose the trophy which the popular Glenn Curtiss had brought to the United States only a year before. Yet even they could not but admire the audacity and determination of the Englishman, Claude Grahame-White.

Flying at the same time as Grahame-White was another Englishman, Thomas Sopwith, who later founded his own airplane building company. Tommy Sopwith, as he was known wherever he went, first flew as a passenger at Brooklands motor-racing track which had become a center for flying and a training school. "I first got the bug," he said, "when I saw the American Moisant flying from Paris to London."

Sopwith bought a monoplane, crashed it, bought another plane—a Howard-Wright biplane—and flew again. He taught himself to fly, qualified as a pilot in November 1910, and then proceeded to win substantial prizes to pay his way. He surprised British flying circles by winning the Baron de Forest prize of $20,000 for the longest flight from England when he flew to Thirlmont in Belgium, 169 miles, and then, with more enthusiasm than experience, took his plane to the United States for further conquests. Unknown when he arrived, Sopwith amazed America by winning more and more money prizes before returning to England.

This was a great period for Tommy Sopwith. He started the Sopwith Company, taught the Australian Harry Hawker to fly, and then employed him as his chief pilot. Sopwith and Hawker were a great combination, and when World War I burst upon the world, it was Sopwith who made his name famous with various Sopwith machines. By the end of hostilities, his Sopwith Camel was legendary in fame. No other Englishman made a greater contribution to international aviation, but it was Reims which gave Sopwith his first enthusiasm for flying and encouraged him to get into this exciting euphoria of aeronautics which was gripping the world.

The French contingent returned home from the second Gordon Bennett Race surprised and sadder but not ashamed. It was part of an aviator's life, and there would still be another year. Since Reims, the previous year, new pilots were appearing on the national scene. There were many older pilots as well who had not flown at Reims yet still fought for recognition. One of these, who had flown in 1908, was Ambrose Goupy who, after working with Voisin to build a triplane and then with Blériot on monoplanes, had recently taken to building biplanes.

Reims was instrumental in bringing many newcomers into flying. Most were Frenchmen, but there were many on both sides of the Atlantic who were not. Two of the most noted French nationals unable to take part at Reims were Trajan Vuia, an Austro-Hungarian lawyer living in Paris, and Édouard de Nieuport. Vuia had taken up engineering but turned to aeronautics for a hobby. In 1905 Vuia suffered many setbacks in his original designs of flying machines but was determined to fly. He continued building his Vuia batlike machine with bicycle-type undercarriage and a wingspan of twenty-eight feet. Despite his energies and undoubted zeal, Vuia lacked technical experience, and although his ideas in 1907 no doubt influenced Louis Blériot and others to concentrate on the monoplane, little was heard of him in the years that followed.

With Vuia fading early from the French scene, Édouard de Nieuport made his appearance. He soon dominated French aviation circles and in World War I his Nieuport was firmly established as one of the most reliable and speediest planes. In 1910, to demonstrate his superiority, Nieuport brought his first monoplane into the open. It was one of the fastest aircraft at the time, with only a 20-horsepower engine, but capable of traveling at 45 miles an hour. What made it so surprising was its completely covered fuselage. The pilot more or less crawled into his cockpit through a small side door until only his head showed above the canvas covering. It was flown by Nieuport at Reims in 1910. The Nieuport monoplane was the forerunner of the World War I "fighter-scout" and made history—like the Deperdussin and the Avro—by protecting the pilot from the buffeting wind and driving rain when in flight. Speeds were increasing, and no longer could a pilot be expected to sit exposed to the elements when flying at 60 or more miles an hour, yet the completely enclosed cockpit was still many years away.

The following March, Nieuport, always striving to bring out something better, produced the latest in airplanes, his type IIN with only a 28-horsepower engine. Nevertheless, this plane was soon to beat the world record and fly at a speed of over 75 miles an hour, which was achieved when he replaced the smaller engines with Gnomes of 70 to 100 horsepower. The year 1911 was a good, yet fatal, one for Nieuport. He again beat the world speed record, with an 83 miles an hour, and later finished third in that year's

Gordon Bennett Race in England. A flying accident on September 15 brought his short but masterly career to a sudden close, and France suffered a great loss by his death.

La Grande Semaine de Reims pour la Champagne lived on. It was not finished at sunset on August 29, 1909. If it could be so termed, it was merely the end of the beginning and the commencement of a new age. For the next two years the interest in flying was amazing. Still in its infancy, flying was spreading across the world. It had begun when the internal combustion engine brought new motive power to transform man-carrying kites into mechanical flight. It continued when aerial races gave man an opportunity to challenge others for speed and endurance. Short races gave place to longer ones, and competitive cross-country flights became popular with money prizes as the inducement.

The next phase took place in Europe. Planes were becoming streamlined, and the pilot's cockpit was more enclosed to protect him from the bitter numbing cold. Following the exposition at Reims, 1910 and 1911 were years of fantastic progress. The appearance of the Deperdussin monoplane in France was the herald of the future, with only the head of the pilot showing behind a protective screened panel. Its slick streamlined appearance, the product of Armand Deperdussin, was the forerunner of the modern plane. It was the first of its kind and indirectly was the result of the competitive events at Reims.

Many such races were held during the months following Reims. Most were small local events, to attract the crowd and make money for the sponsors who cared little for the progress of aviation except when it would benefit them. But the officially sponsored aviation meetings, like those held under the auspices of the American, French, and British Aero Clubs, were different. Their object was solely

to promote flying, and by such races as the Gordon Bennett
Trophy and other international competitions they encouraged aircraft builders to improve their machines by new
and better designs—and make it advantageous for pilots to
fly them. The cross-country flights for competing men and
planes, like the circuits of Europe, of Great Britain,
and elsewhere, some lesser in name but as important in
character, were all the result of that memorable meeting at
Reims in the summer of 1909.

It is not possible to describe all the meetings, the races,
and the aeronautical trials that took place during the following years of 1910 and 1911, crucial years in aviation.
The Gordon Bennett Race of 1910, which took place at
Belmont Park, New York, was the highlight that year. In
1911 two great events gave flying an impetus that was un-
precedented, the Circuit of Europe and the Circuit of
Britain. To succeed, aircraft builders devoted their energies,
time, and money to make their airplanes faster and more
durable in bad weather, and the engine makers concentrated on improved and more powerful motive power.

Pilots, too, with the added experience of Reims and public demonstrations of flying, became more daring in their
efforts to prove the progress of aviation. One historic milestone was the American International Meeting at the Belmont racetrack in New York. While it did not prove to be
the great success that was anticipated, due to a dissension
between those flying and the committee who organized the
meeting, the public were given an exhibition of faster and
more positive aerial display.

The second Gordon Bennett Trophy Race was like the
first at Reims, full of thrills and excitement. The meeting
began on Saturday, October 29, 1910, when teams from
France and Britain vied with the best of American fliers to
capture the coveted trophy. The first day was not ideal

flying weather. It seemed to follow the Reims pattern. It rained during the night with fog at sunrise, but as the sun rose, a treacherous wind swept across the course making takeoff and landing a dangerous hazard. During the morning the wind dropped, and everyone was pleased to see the planes wheeled out of the hangars and the spectators given their first thrills of flying.

The second Gordon Bennett Trophy was to be the greatest race ever flown. The rules had been changed somewhat. There would be twenty laps of the 5-kilometer course, and flying must be between 8:30 A.M. and 3:30 P.M. The American contestants were Charles K. Hamilton in a Curtiss 110-horsepower, and Walter Brookins for the Wrights in their new *Baby Grand* 60-horsepower. The French had Hubert Latham, now flying a 100-horsepower Antoinette, Leblanc in a 100-horsepower Blériot, and Eugène Aubrun in a smaller Blériot. For Britain, besides Grahame-White, there were two others, both in smaller machines.

Now, only a year after Reims, airplanes were beginning to acquire stability. New designs were appearing; the old flimsy materials were giving place to stronger and more durable components. Pilots were more daring and prepared to fly higher and faster; engines had been improved with extra power, power that was necessary if steady progress was to be expected. It was still a risk to take a plane off the ground, engines still failed but less frequently, and if pilots exercised care, accidents could be avoided.

The Wright brothers still exerted a strong influence on flying. When they themselves took no active part, the men they had taught to fly were showing what was necessary for success. As at Reims, the Gordon Bennett Trophy had become the most important race, and everyone, pilots and public, looked forward to this with growing excitement.

The first day's flying was marred by one serious crash when
Tod Shriver dived to earth from fifty feet and wrecked his
Dietz biplane. He was unhurt, but the plane was badly
damaged. Unlike Reims, there were no failures with planes
unable to rise from the ground; every plane was able to
take off and demonstrate its airworthiness.

A noticeable arrival was the new Wright biplane built
for speed. It immediately became a center of interest. It
was smaller than their standard machine, smaller than the
Curtiss plane that had won at Reims the previous year,
being 21 feet 6 inches in span and the wings 3 feet in width.
Fitted with a 65-horsepower engine, it was expected to beat
all the others for speed and maneuverability.

To add to the enjoyment, one spectator arrived by air.
It was Captain Baldwin, one of the first men to fly. He had
built his own plane and now was able to demonstrate the
practicability of air transport. He lived less than ten miles
away, but his arrival was significant. After circling the
ground, he dropped slowly toward the center of the field and
landed without incident, as though it were an everyday occurrence.

Each day of the meeting provided thrills. The 500-feet
record of Reims was long forgotten when Ralph Johnstone
flew to over 7,300 feet—how much higher could man fly?
In the speed events Latham flew his Antoinette monoplane
at 65 miles an hour. The next day Orville Wright, determined to show how fast he could fly, clocked his biplane at
70 miles an hour. So it went on with growing excitement
until the great day arrived when the second Gordon Bennett
Race would be decided.

The rules for flying were becoming more and more strin-
gent. Contestants would not be allowed to pass another at
less than a minimum distance of 75 feet or pass over him at
less than 150 feet. Pilots would not be permitted to fly over

the public and the stands. Landing and taking off would now be regulated and no plane allowed to remain in the center of the field.

The closing scenes were reminiscent of Reims as the race for the Gordon Bennett Trophy was being concluded. Grahame-White completed the twenty circuits—each of 5 kilometers, 62 miles—in 1 hour 1 minute 4.5 seconds, a little over 60 miles an hour.

The Frenchman Leblanc then took off in his Blériot monoplane and immediately showed a faster time for the first circuit. By the end of nineteen laps he was well ahead of Grahame-White, an astonishing 5½ minutes. Then disaster occurred. To save weight, sacrificing gasoline for greater speed, Leblanc miscalculated badly. When only one circuit short of the full distance, his gasoline supply suddenly ran out and he dived into the ground. Smashing into a telegraph pole, his machine was a complete wreck, but Leblanc escaped with only scratches on his face and bruises on the body.

With Leblanc out of the race, Ogilvie was the next to takeoff, but the American's time was too slow for this important event—he could do no better than 52 miles an hour. Another accident occurred when Brookins in his *Baby Grand* was caught in a crosswind and crashed from two hundred feet, but he, too, was unhurt, and managed to climb out of the wreckage. The last to fly were John Moisant and J. Armstrong Drexel, both in Blériot monoplanes and both hopeful of keeping the cup in America, but they failed, Drexel giving up after seven laps and Moisant unable to beat Graham-White's time.

This was not to be a repetition of the 1909 race. Although Blériot failed when he had the previous year's race in his grasp, his planes secured the honors for speed and reliability which the Wright brothers were unable to do at Belmont Park. The 1910 race saw the specially designed and hastily built Blériot monoplane, flown by Grahame-White, far ahead of any rival. Against the record time of a minute or so over the hour for the twenty 5-kilometer laps, Moisant was only able to return a time of 1 hour 57 minutes 45 seconds. His speed of 31½ miles an hour, while giving him second place, showed the great difference between the two fliers.

In a little over a year since the first meeting at Reims, history recorded little headway in speed. To fly at 70 miles an hour, conditions had to be near perfect and only for a short flight. But what was apparent was the reliability of aircraft when flown carefully and without taking unnecessary risks. Pilots could fly longer and higher, cross-country flights were commonplace, and new records for heights demonstrated the daring and determination of individual men. From a mere 500 feet in August 1909 the world record had risen to 9,714 feet set by an American, Johnstone, before the end of 1910. Another American, Drexel, had taken his plane up to 9,450 feet before the cold and rarefied air forced him to return. (Drexel's attempt was first given as 9,970 feet, but when the sealed barograph was officially examined, the lower height was substituted.) Both these heights showed what man could do and what strides had been made in those years of 1909 and 1910.

Airplane designs were changing rapidly. Air resistance was reduced wherever possible, while engine horsepower was increased to give greater speed. The monoplane was beginning to assert its superiority over the biplane, yet both were still built of spruce and ash with the occasional use of tubular steel for the main structural members. Wings were still covered with varnished cotton fabric, and the propeller was mahogany, but the cockpit floor now had a plywood covering which made flying more comfortable.

The cross-country races in Europe during 1910 and 1911 produced a remarkable assembly of pilots and showed the advance of aeronautics to an astonishing degree. The principal race in 1911—less than two years after Reims —was therefore not altogether surprising. There were over forty planes competing, including C. T. Weymann from the United States. Of these, only six were biplanes—three being Farman's, of a new design.

The favorites were Lieutenant Jean Conneau, flying under the name of André Beaumont, as he was a serving officer, and Roland Garros, Blériot's onetime head mechanic and now his best flier. They were both flying Blériots. Monsieur Vidart had a Deperdussin, as also had Maurice Prévost and the Englishman Jimmy Valentine, while of the others Monsieur Kimmerling flying a Sommer was expected to do well. Eugène Gilbert, in an R.E.P., a failure at Reims but now redesigned, was equally favored.

It was a wonderful race and remembered by all who saw it as the planes passed overhead or as they landed at the intermediate stops. It was an unforgettable sight of aerial progress. It started on June 18 from the Vincennes Champ de Manoeuvre and was scheduled to last three weeks. The course was a long one for those early days of flying. Paris, Liège, Utrecht, Brussels, Roubaix, Calais, then over the English Channel to Shoreham, where they rested. From there they would fly to London and then return to France via Calais direct to Paris, a distance of 1,200 miles.

What a race it became! Nothing like this had ever been attempted before. Flying in unpredictable weather, gales, rainstorms, and even snow, in open cockpits (if the canvas-screened area could be called that), and only three weeks in which to complete the course. Yet twenty-one planes reached Liège in Belgium.

The start of the race was disastrous. Many planes crashed at takeoff; three men were killed and several other pilots injured, one seriously. Some hit the trees surrounding the Champ de Manoeuvre, others failed to lift their planes off the ground. It was not a happy day for those watching or for the officials who had organized the race. Yet it was thrilling, in spite of the crashes, to see the more fortunate pilots lift off their planes into the air, clear the trees, and gradually fade into the distance as they sped on their way.

The race was soon narrowed to a contest between four Frenchmen—the naval lieutenant, Conneau (Beaumont), Jules Vedrines, Garros, and Vidart. Beaumont in a Blériot introduced new ideas for cross-country flying. With naval training he flew for the first time guided by landmarks, some familiar no doubt, and by compass on a plotted course. There was Vedrines in a new Morane monoplane. He had been a mechanic with the Gnome Engine Company but now, like Farman, was becoming one of the leading French fliers. Garros, who had been a mechanic with Louis Blériot, was another newcomer as a leading pilot. These were the pilots who were taking the places vacated by Blériot, Latham, Paulhan, and the rest; new planes and new faces. Garros was a pilot in his own right, flying a Blériot monoplane with a 50-horsepower Gnome engine. Vidart was a comparative newcomer but showing a natural instinct for handling aircraft. He was flying the latest Deperdussin, also with a 50-horsepower engine. So the "Round Europe Race" started.

Beaumont was the first away at ten o'clock, followed by Garros, Vidart, Vedrines, and the rest. It was not long before the race became a close fight between these four men, with Beaumont never far out of the lead. The excitement grew as each stage was completed. Most of the competitors had previously won at least one race of importance, which made the European Circuit Race headline news.

By July 2, there were eleven pilots at Calais waiting to leave the following day. Fourteen had arrived in Holland, but with mishaps and errors in cross-country flying, the number was being reduced daily. The race had now become a fight between a few—all experienced—fliers, and so it continued day by day.

By the evening of the next day all eleven fliers had crossed the English Channel. To men like Blériot it was an amazing sight. Only two years before he was the first to accomplish this feat, and now a host of pilots were making the crossing like a flight of birds migrating. "It is madness," he exclaimed. "How many will return. . . . This is not a race, it is nonsense."

Race or nonsense, the British crowds who awaited the arrival of the aviators at Hendon Field in London had other feelings. Above the field to guide the fliers in their approach was a captive balloon, pink in the morning sun.

Suddenly there was a shout, "There it is—over there. It's coming in to land. . . ."

The speck grew larger as the shouting increased. It took shape as it swept across the field and landed as though it were an everyday occurrence. It was Vedrines in his Morane monoplane. He had left Calais at 4 A.M., and after stopping briefly at Dover and Shoreham airfields on the English Coast for official checking, he had continued his flight to reach the halfway point of London only four and a half hours later. This intense flying was a revelation to everyone. Others were arriving now, Vidart, Gilbert, and the favorite—Beaumont—fourth. Coming singly, not many

minutes apart, the excitement grew. While the crowd of
early spectators was getting over the first surprise, five
more planes arrived en masse—"a flock of them," as
someone described their arrival. Before long eleven planes
were on the ground or in the hangars, with mechanics
working like ants to have each machine ready for its
next flight. But the last of the arrivals were quickly surrounded by a mob of enthusiasts, with the police helpless
to control the crowd.

The later pilots told their stories of mistaken bearings
and unforeseen troubles—some far off course, others
having just bad luck. While Vedrines had arrived to find
the field almost empty, the news of his arrival spread
quickly to the surrounding districts. Within half an hour,
while the others were still arriving, the field was crowded
with an excited mass of spectators, cheering each pilot
as he arrived. The Channel-crossing stage had ended
without serious trouble, and the planes were soon over-
hauled and repaired in readiness for the return flight three
days later. These three days were the "official" rest period.
Exhibition flights by Beaumont, Garros, Vedrines, and
others gave Londoners many an unexpected thrill. Grahame-White, one of the organizers not contesting, demonstrated his latest machine and added to the excitement
of the onlookers.

Wednesday morning came for the return flight. The
pilots were up early, the sky was cloudy, the air cold as
dawn gave way to early morning light. Almost to the
minute Beaumont was the first to leave, with Garros and
the others tailing him into the air. Forty miles south of
London they were almost together, flying only a few hundred feet above the ground. Some looked like eagles as
they roared overhead, while others, cumbersome structures
of canvas-covered frames, flew their course as freaks of

man's imagination to defeat gravitation. The race, to onlookers waiting in country fields, on hilltops or standing
outside their houses in the towns en route, seemed over
almost as soon as it started. From the first shout as
Beaumont was sighted, specks in the sky developed into
man-carrying machines; a few minutes of roaring engines
as they passed overhead and then they were on their way,
disappearing from sight in the misty overcast. That was
the brief experience by onlookers of the greatest race of
the year—the European Circuit.

Thursday was devoted solely to the return cross-Channel flight. They crossed the English Channel as the sun
rose. Vedrines led the way. This time the wind was
favorable, and he passed over the narrow strip of water
in just over half an hour. Eight others also made the
hop, with the slowest less than twenty minutes behind
Vedrines. Their close flying was remarkable, and with
only two pilots delayed by minor troubles, the satisfactory
flight by the remaining airmen was phenomenal.

The last stage was the most dramatic. From Calais
they were to fly to Paris, with a brief check at Amiens.
They arrived well within schedule. Vincennes airfield was
crowded with the top army and government personages
on hand to welcome the winners. The planes were early,
the first landing at 8:30 A.M. But this did not detract
from the enthusiasm. Out of the haze, one by one they
suddenly appeared overhead. The unmistakable hum of
the engine could be heard before each plane was sighted.
The crowds rushed forward eager to see who was leading.

Was it Vedrines or Beaumont? It was neither. The unknown newcomer, Vidart in a Deperdussin, was first. As
he climbed out of his seat, he was seized and carried
shoulder high toward the grandstand to the rousing tune
of the "Marseillaise." Seven minutes later came another,

Gilbert, almost as unknown as Vidart. Gilbert, though, had the distinction of being the only competitor who had flown the same machine throughout; the others had changed planes when necessary. At last came the popular ones— Garros, third, and Beaumont, the favorite, fourth. Where was Vedrines? Where was the leader? The answer was soon forthcoming. He had damaged his Morane monoplane on landing at Amiens but was still in the race.

It is dramatic how the flying order can change under such conditions. Engine trouble, even the slighest mishap, and valuable time could be lost before the race could be continued. So with Vedrines: a leader almost from the start, he would now be lucky to finish in the first ten or finish at all. And so to Paris.

Only the judges could give the verdict calculated on points, and this came when the day's flying was over and all contestants were down. Beaumont, Lieutenant Conneau, was declared the winner with a flying time of 58 hours 38 minutes, only 3½ hours less than the runner-up, Roland Garros—Blériot's onetime mechanic. The success of the two Blériot monoplanes in this three-weeks struggle for survival and achievement gave the great pioneer much satisfaction and prestige in international flying circles. From motorcar lamp manufacturer to airplane builder, winner of many races, to flying instructor and organizer, he had seen the two top places in the greatest long-distance race ever to be flown taken by his own monoplanes. This was Blériot's greatest day since his Channel crossing and success at Reims in 1909 only two years before.

The Achievements of Reims

What really was achieved at Reims? What benefits came out of the meeting, and what was happening throughout the world in immediate years following this first international event? That it was a success there is no doubt, and governments were now taking a fresh look at aviation. It was no longer another form of amusement for a few wealthy playboys but a new mode of transport that could become a major industry. Visitors to Reims were returning seriously impressed with what they had seen; the military and naval attachés were reporting on the possibilities which aviation could bring to modern warfare, and bankers and financiers, too, were taking a fresh look at the problems involved. The United States was no exception. Washington was no longer apathetic, and the pioneers Wilbur and Orville Wright, and now Curtiss, would no longer have to wait in outer offices, cap in hand, waiting for something to happen.

Glenn Curtiss returned in triumph to Hammondsport. With orders pouring in, the Curtiss Company, like the

Wright Corporation, became the center of much activity. Apart from the ever-present patent arguments with the Wrights, Glenn Curtiss had no problems. His time now was spent in designing and building newer and better airplanes. His Curtiss biplane had put him on a pinnacle of fame and he was making the most of it. After Reims, he made a quick journey to Italy to fly a Brescia, where he added more prizes to his collection. His visit to Europe had been more than paid for—expenses were met with plenty to spare. Although he never again made such a spectacular triumph as at Reims, he returned full of optimism for the business he had founded at Hammondsport.

His wife was urging him to give up active flying. "Let others do that," she advised him. "The company is more important than demonstrations at airfields. Leave that to others. Train the younger men to fly. There are so many who are eager to fly but have no one to train them or airplanes to fly in."

It was true, and when Curtiss surveyed the situation after only a few weeks abroad, he realized the necessity of concentrating on the manufacturing side of his life and leaving active flying to others.

Much had happened while he was away. The patent situation had worsened; the Wright brothers and their financial advisers were trying to prevent him and anyone else from flying unless royalties on their "wing warping" patents were paid. They claimed a monopoly and threatened to stop him flying or even making airplanes without their permission. It was a crucial period for American aviation.

Other men were making the news headlines. More and greater interest in flying was spreading across the United States. From New York to California, the success of Reims was creating a demand for similar flying meetings in every community where money could be found available to attract the fliers and their machines. The year 1910 was a great one for American flying, and this outburst of interest following the gliding days of Chanute and the Wrights to one of the exciting demonstrations of powered flying would be continued into 1911 and beyond.

This change of attitude had started in February 1909, when Joseph Pulitzer, owner of the New York *World,* made a startling offer which had almost been forgotten— a prize of $10,000 to the first to fly between New York and Albany in either direction. It was not original; it had followed other generous offers made earlier by such news- men as Lord Northcliffe, of the *Daily Mail* in London, and James Gordon Bennett, of the New York *Herald,* but it was the first time that a competitive event had been suggested for the United States, far removed from the European scene. As no one was ready in 1909 to fly the stipulated course, Pulitzer extended the time limit to Octo- ber 1910.

This was Curtiss's last great flight, and he made headline news with his success. It was not the distance that was the obstacle, but the treacherous winds, which could cause disaster, blowing down the river between the mountains. It was a challenge that Curtiss could not resist, and he was soon making preparations for the 150-mile flight to Governors Island. Curtiss's predilection for planning and unwillingness to take chances were not surprising, but what amazed everyone was the speed and simplicity with which, in those early days, he completed the flight. After Reims he built a new airplane which he called *The Albany Flyer,* and to this he fitted a float made out of rubberized cloth and filled with granules of cork to aid the buoyancy of the machine if it had to alight on the water. The new plane had one of Curtiss's new 8-cylinder 50-horsepower engines, air-cooled to save weight.

When news of his intending flight leaked out, others quickly followed suit. Their intended presence worried Curtiss, yet, as always, he was not to be hurried. He knew they could not take part in such a race without much preparation, and in this he was correct. First on the scene, he was the first to get away, and while the city slept that Sunday morning of May 29, Curtiss had *The Albany Flyer* rolled out of its tent on Van Rensselaer Island. Long before the church bells of Albany were ringing, while most people were still in bed, Curtiss was in the air and heading down the Hudson River for his distant goal. One brief stop near Poughkeepsie for gasoline and oil and he was off again. Less than two and a half hours from the time of leaving Albany, Curtiss was over New York City. He stopped near 214th Street to repair a leaking oil-tank line, but with oil and gasoline replenished, he was soon off again.

Flying over Manhattan, circling the Statue of Liberty and crossing the short stretch of water with every ship, tug, and launch blowing whistles to welcome his arrival, Curtiss gave New Yorkers one of the best demonstrations that they were ever likely to see. He landed on Governors Island nine minutes before noon, to the cheers of the military garrison after 2 hours 46 minutes of actual flying time. What amazed everyone was his speed of over 54 miles an hour. It was a stupendous flight, and when Curtiss and his wife went to the Astor Hotel in Times Square for lunch that same day, New Yorkers went wild.

On the way to Times Square, Curtiss called at City Hall to deliver a letter of greeting from the mayor of Albany to the mayor of New York. It was a historic act. Dated May 29, 1910, that letter inaugurated the United States Air Mail Service.

The Albany–New York flight not only added luster to Curtiss's many earlier achievements but awakened the public's interest to what flying could do for them and the world. With the sole exception of Wilbur and Orville Wright, Curtiss probably did more for American flying than anyone else. It was Glenn Curtiss's accomplishments, his flights, and his demonstrations of speed and safety combined that made possible the fast and sure progress of that first decade following the original powered flight at Kitty Hawk.

By 1910, the American aeronautical scene was beginning to change. Dominated as it had been by the Wrights and Curtiss, others were forcing their way to recognition. Apart from the few who were being taught to fly at Dayton or Hammondsport, the Midwest and West had others whose names were making news.

In 1907 a young man named Glenn L. Martin built his first heavier-than-air machine, a monoplane with many original features. Like the Wrights and Curtiss and so many others in France and elsewhere, Martin had started his life's work as a motor mechanic. His first attempt at flying was a complete failure, and he gathered up the remains of the machine with a determination to build another. In the summer of 1909—when Curtiss was preparing to leave for Reims—Glenn Martin, with his mother as his only aid, wheeled out his first airplane into the California sunlight. That flight on August 1 of only one hundred feet brought Glenn Martin into the exclusive group—now three—of aircraft builders in the United States. His short flight showed without doubt that others were capable of building and flying an airplane.

Glenn Martin was convinced that his future lay in building aircraft and looked around for money to fulfill his ambitions. With that first plane now strengthened and

powered for demonstration flying, he began his quest for
finance wherewith to start his company. He traveled anywhere if the money was sufficiently attractive. He was
frugal, never losing sight of his objective and returning to
California whenever possible to make another step forward
toward starting his own company. Two years later, in
1911, he incorporated his own company and was soon
ranked with the Wrights and Curtiss as an aircraft builder
of repute. He continued to give flights to those who were
willing to pay and although never a spectacular flier, at
last fulfilled his ambition by creating the Martin Aircraft
—a name which still survives.

These three years, 1909, 1910, and 1911, while being
years of triumph were also years of disappointment to
those seeking to develop the aircraft industry. The wheels
of bureaucracy turned far too slowly and too late. Not
enough money was forthcoming to meet the trials and
development costs. Early aviators met with dilatoriness,
doubts, and the outright opposition and scorn of the holders
of the nation's purse strings in Washington. They were to
blame for the absence of American-made aircraft over
the battlefields of Europe during World War I. It is an
incredible fact that the country where the first powered
flight was made in 1903 by the Wright brothers, where
Curtiss, Martin, and others were flying not many years
later, was not ready to build fighter aircraft for the United
States Air Force pilots to fly in France in 1917 and 1918.

By 1910 American aircraft industries were taking shape.
Not only was Glenn Martin making dramatic headway in
airplane building, but there were others such as Allan
Lougheed, who had been working for Martin. When Lougheed changed the name of his own company to Lockheed
for easier spelling, he started a chain of events that subsequently made a great impact on the new industry. Another

staff member was the later independent designer John K. Northrop. He sold a plane to an engineer in Seattle named William E. Boeing, and later gave Donald Douglas, Sr., a job in his works. Glenn Martin proved by helping others that competition is an aid to progress and not a hindrance. If by giving Lougheed employment in the newly started airplane industry was not enough, he also gave Lawrence D. Bell and J. A. Kindelberger jobs on his designing staff. Both men started their own companies, Bell under his own name, and Kindelberger the North American Aviation Company. The lives of all these men, like so many before and since, show what can be done when man has an idea and is willing to work under adverse conditions to achieve success.

Clyde Cessna from Kansas was another American pioneer. Late in 1910 he finished his first plane, taking it to Oklahoma, where he hoped to test its flying capabilities. Like most early builders of heavier-than-air machines, Cessna's first plane was not a success. It was underpowered, not strong enough to support its own weight when landing, and capable of flying only in short hops. As Cessna said at the time: "I had many heartbreaking experiences; trials and wrecks . . . money for food often went on necessary repairs, but I kept on. I just knew I could make a small but useful airplane that anyone could fly."

Building airplanes was one thing, but flying them was something else. Putting ideas into practice meant, in those days, risking one's life for popularity, for the thrill and pleasure of rising from the ground and circling above a field of excited people. A few pilots were already wealthy, others were able to make a good living by winning money prizes, but some—as history records—became famous for a while, then crashed and were soon forgotten. As they vanished from the scene, others appeared to take their place.

The earliest of these fliers were Wright-trained Walter Brookins and Arch Hoxsey. There was Duval La Chappelle, who had worked for Wilbur Wright in France as a mechanic, Ralph Johnstone, Frank Coffyn, and A. L. Welsh. What a group! It included the son of a New York banker, an automobile racer, a trick bicycle rider, and a part-time circus clown. Together they made a great name as the "Wright Barnstorming Group," but individually they were natural-born fliers who were soon recognized wherever they went for their wonderful flying demonstrations and thrills. Their activities led to Wilbur's direct injunction to Johnstone and Hoxsey (the Frenchman Lefebvre had already killed himself making unnecessarily dangerous flights): "I want no stunts and spectacular flights. Make a plain flight of, say, fifteen minutes a day—well away from the grandstand and never over three hundred feet high." But they, like others, only remembered his instructions for a while until, with familiarity breeding contempt, they soon returned to their risky stunts.

The first to go was Johnstone who, seeing Hoxsey making spectacular dips and climbs in front of the grandstand, decided to emulate his example and, if possible, make an even more startling flight. He climbed to 800 feet and began a spiral glide toward the field. But this time, at the last moment, the plane failed to respond to the controls, and Johnstone was killed in the resulting crash. Six weeks later Hoxsey, attempting to beat the world's new altitude record of 11,474 feet (a year earlier at Reims Latham's world record was 508 feet!), gave up the attempt and started stunting a few hundred feet above the ground until a gusty wind forced him downward. The machine was wrecked as it hit the ground in a series of somersaults, and Hoxsey's body was found in the wreckage. While the public was recovering from these tragedies, a third, John Moisant, one of the leading American prize winners of 1910, crashed while flying in New Orleans on December 31. He was killed instantly.

These and other deaths, some quite needlessly, tolled the bell for "barnstorming" as a big attraction. The newspapers protested over the unnecessary deaths. Flying should be taken more seriously, they told their readers—"There are greater things ahead for aviation."

Fun there always will be, foolish people come and go, but these deaths sobered others to more careful flying and brought a more sensible approach. One of these more sensible fliers was Lincoln Beachey. He had once flown dirigibles with Thomas Baldwin in 1905 and had flown the gas-filled lighter-than-air balloons across the country until he took to powered flight. It was therefore no surprise to find in him a careful pilot who took no chances and no liberties with his machine.

When Beachey joined Glenn Curtiss as a mechanic and was taught by him to fly, he was only twenty-three, and Curtiss was hesitant about Beachey's future. "Always breaking something, a wheel, a wing tip, or an undercarriage," said Curtiss, "yet in spite of my doubts about his ever being able to fly, I had the feeling he was a born flier."

Curtiss was proved right, and Lincoln Beachey went on to become one of the best of the early fliers during 1910 and 1911. He helped to prove that the Curtiss plane was well built, reliable, and fast. What more could Curtiss want? Beachey flew in Florida and through all the eastern states. He gave crowds in Washington, D.C., thrills and excitement as he flew over the city, circling the Capitol and the White House, with a characteristic style that pleased almost everyone. Yet even Beachey knew how dangerous flying could be when it seemed impossible for the frail structure of wires, wood, and canvas to survive. He flew over Niagara Falls and underneath the bridge, a few hundred yards from where the water tumbles over in a cloud of spray. He flew through the spray and close to the whirling rapids, through the gusty winds in the narrow gorge, and again survived.

In the upsurge of flying that occurred in 1911, more and more pilots were being killed as the months went by. Beachey's daring led many, who had only a fraction of his experience, to attempt similar feats, but only a few could emulate his success. By 1911, the two big manufacturers, the Wright brothers and Curtiss, were calling a halt to this drama of death. The reason was quickly obvious: the Army and Navy were getting worried, and dare not continue their interest in flying, since they could not afford to lose good officers in crashes; injuries and death played no part in their plans. No government department could allow stunts or dangerous flying; they were only interested in defensive or, if necessary, offensive flying and all that it might resolve. The edict of the American Aero Club and its affiliated members was clear and final: "Only well-organized and stunt-free meetings would be permitted."

During 1911 the center of competitive flying moved back to Europe. England, in 1911, was to be the venue of the Gordon Bennett Race. Grahame-White was the holder of the trophy and, as such, was now to defend his title in his own country.

The atmosphere was different from the novelty of Reims in 1909 and the ebullient, excited, and controversial Belmont Park of 1910. The third meeting was held in England in an atmosphere of calm. The race for the world speed record over a set course was dispassionate, yet intensely competitive. Fighting hard, this time with many new faces, the United States flying team arrived, hopeful of regaining the trophy.

C. T. Weymann was America's principal hope. Unknown at the time of the first Reims meeting, Weymann made a name for himself the following year at several air shows in the United States. Weymann deserved his inclusion in the team, and at Eastchurch, in southeast England, fifty miles from the congested suburbs of London, he showed his superiority by winning the cup in a French machine designed and constructed in America against the best French and British pilots. He piloted his Nieuport monoplane from first to last in the style of a champion. Even Nieuport, in his own similarly designed and built machine, could not equal Weymann's performance.

Blériot, too, showed he was still a force to be reckoned with, and when Leblanc in his Blériot followed Weymann, the old pioneer proved he had progressed with the best of the newcomers in world aviation. The race was over 94 miles—each year had seen an increase in the distance—but now each machine was a proven piece of apparatus. Gone were the frail uncertain structures of previous years; they were now fast and reliable when handled with skill. What a change after Reims only two years earlier. Racing had improved beyond recognition. Pilots and airplane builders were learning by bitter experience, and at last flying was beginning to enter an era of safety.

Speed, while not all-important, still played a part in international and well-organized events. This was shown at Eastchurch in England when the third Gordon Bennett Race was held. Weymann's speed was phenomenal. He flashed across the finishing line after 1 hour 11 minutes 36.2 seconds of daring flying at an average speed of 78 miles an hour. It was enough to win him the trophy in spite

of the close finishing efforts of the two top French pilots—
Leblanc and Nieuport. This was the second time Leblanc
had failed to win the Gordon Bennett Race. The previous
year he had crashed while beating Grahame-White's time,
and now he had lost again. But now he was to lose by only
1 minute 55 seconds, with Nieuport a mere 57 seconds
behind. This was remarkable flying with only 3 minutes
separating the first three pilots over a course of nearly 100
miles, with speeds of 78, 76, and 75 miles an hour. It had
been a fine win for the United States and showed, with
Weymann flying a Nieuport like the other two, that France
could still build fast and dependable machines even if they
could not win this famous race.

Weymann's success proved one thing, that it was the man
at the controls who counted and not the machine. True it
was that the annual Gordon Bennett event was still attract-
ing international attention, but it was slowly becoming
apparent that speed was not the only requisite. The mere
circling of an airfield to demonstrate an airplane's capabilities, to show how fast it could go, was not enough. The
airplane could be used for more practical purposes: people
would soon want to travel by the shortest route between
cities, and freight, even mail, could be carried. Such possibilities were now being envisaged and this at a time when
airplanes were still being constructed of ash, spruce, and
some steel tubes covered with varnished cotton fabric and
held together with steel wire.

Science was at last taking a hand in the advancement of
the industry. What was needed was a stable machine, easy
to control, with power to carry quantities of freight or a
number of passengers, or both, with speed to improve on
the slower modes of travel on the ground. This was basically
what the individual international aero clubs had set out to

do and, indirectly through Reims and other worldwide competitions, sought for the benefit of aviation.

Gradually it was being demonstrated that the airplane was capable of traversing great distances, of flying high above the storms and cloud cover near the ground. Reims and other meetings proved that long-distance races could be won by an entrant who made his plans carefully, organized his supplies, used the best equipment, and kept the machine in perfect or near-perfect condition.

At first the story of flight was told through pioneers who had to battle with all forms of adversity, to finance their work out of their own pockets, and to make progress slowly, sometimes with bitter results, to achieve some measure of success. With the advent of Reims, inducing publicity-seeking corporations and newspaper publishers to give money prizes, such men as Curtiss, the Wrights, Blériot, and Farman found it possible to carry on the work they and others had started and to secure a place for themselves in the flying industry.

Three criteria for success in flying came out of the "flying week" at Reims: reliability of motive power, strength and durability in design and materials, and sound judgment by the pilot. All three had to be combined in order to conquer flight, and this could be accomplished only by continuing the spirit of Reims—the camaraderie of pilots, mechanics, designers, and aircraft builders. Human frailty would always be present, accidents would occur—they would be inevitable—but only by testing one plane against another, one man's ideas against something different, could flying become a safe pursuit and a new mode of transport for the world.

Bibliography

Dolfus, Charles, and Bouché, Henri. *Histoire de l'Aéronautique.* Paris: L'Illustration, 1942.

Gibbs-Smith, C. H. *A Brief History of Flying.* London: H.M.S.O., 1967.

———. *The World's First Aeroplane Flights.* London: H.M.S.O., 1965.

———. *The Wright Brothers.* London: H.M.S.O., 1963.

Harris, Sherwood. *The First to Fly.* New York: Simon and Schuster, 1970.

Langley, Samuel P. Langley Memoir on Mechanical Flight. Washington, D.C.: Smithsonian Institution, 1911.

Linecar, Harold. *Early Aeroplanes.* London: Ernest Benn, 1965.

Munson, Kenneth. *Pioneer Aircraft.* London: Blandford Press, 1969.

Santos-Dumont, Alberto. *Dans l'Air.* Paris, 1904.

Scharff, Robert, and Taylor, Walter S. *Over Land and Sea.* New York: David McKay, 1968.

Tuck, W. J. *Power to Fly.* London: H.M.S.O., 1966.

Voisin, Gabriel. *Men, Women, and 10,000 Kites.* Trans. Oliver Stewart. London: Putnam, 1963.

Wallace, Graham. *Claude Grahame-White.* London: Putnam, 1962.

Wykenham, Peter. *Santos-Dumont.* London: Putnam, 1962.

Appendix
Results of Competitive Events
at the Reims
Flying Meeting
1909

Competition Winners

Place	Pilot	Max. dist. flown		Time (hrs.)
		Kilometers	*Miles*	
1	Farman	180	112	3:04:56.0
2	Latham (29)	154	95½	2:18:09.4
3	Paulhan	131	81¼	2:40:00.0
4	De Lambert	116	72	1:50:59.2
5	Latham (13)	111	70	1:38:05.2
6	Tissandier	110	70	1:46:52.0

COUPE GORDON BENNETT (TWO CIRCUITS, 10 KILOMETERS EACH)

Place	Pilot	Time (mins.)		
		1st circuit	*2nd circuit*	*Total*
1	Curtiss	7:57.4	7:53.2	15:50.6
2	Blériot	7:53.2	8:03.0	15:56.2
3	Latham	8:51.0	8:41.0	17:32.0
4	Lefebvre	9:45.8	11:01.8	20:47.6

PRIX DE LA VITESSE (THREE CIRCUITS, 10 KILOMETERS EACH)

Place	Pilot	Total (mins.)
1	Curtiss	23:29.0
2	Latham	25:18.2
3	Tissandier	28:59.2
4	Lefebvre	29:02.0

PRIX DE TOUR DE PISTE (ONE CIRCUIT, 10 KILOMETERS)

Place	Pilot	Best time (mins.)
1	Blériot	7:47.8
2	Curtiss	7:49.4

PRIX DES PASSAGERS (ONE CIRCUIT, 10 KILOMETERS)

Place	Pilot	No. of passengers	Time (mins.)
1	Farman	2	10:39.0
2	Farman	1	9:52.2
3	Lefebvre	1	10:39.0

PRIX DE L'ALTITUDE

Place	Pilot	Heights Reached Meters	Feet
1	Latham	155	508
2	Farman	110	360

World Speed Records at Reims

Distance (kilometers)	Pilot	Time (hrs.)
10	Blériot	0:07:47.6
20	Curtiss	0:15:50.2
30	Curtiss	0:23:29.0
50	Latham	0:43:56.0
100	Latham	1:28:17.0
150	Latham	2:13:09.2

Prize Money Won by Pilots

Farman		*Winnings (Francs)*
1. Grand Prix		50,000
1. Prix des Passagers		10,000
2. Prix de l'Altitude		3,000
	Total	63,000

Latham		
2. Grand Prix		25,000
1. Prix de l'Altitude		7,000
5. Grand Prix		5,000
2. Prix de la Vitesse		5,000
	Total	42,000

Curtiss		
1. Coupe Gordon Bennett		25,000
1. Prix de la Vitesse		10,000
2. Prix de Tour de Piste		3,000
	Total	38,000

Paulhan		
3. Grand Prix		10,000
	Total	10,000

Tissandier		
6. Grand Prix		5,000
3. Prix de la Vitesse		3,000
	Total	8,000

Blériot		
1. Prix de Tour de Piste		7,000
	Total	7,000

De Lambert
4. Grand Prix   5,000
                                        Total   5,000

Lefebvre
4. Prix de la Vitesse   2,000
                                        Total   2,000

Index